Web Page Recommendation Models: Theory and Algorithms
Şule Gündüz-Öğüdücü

ISBN: 978-3-031-00714-9   paperback
ISBN: 978-3-031-01842-8   ebook

DOI 10.1007/978-3-031-01842-8

A Publication in the Springer series
SYNTHESIS LECTURES ON DATA MANAGEMENT

Lecture #10
Series Editor: M. Tamer Özsu, *University of Waterloo*
Series ISSN
Synthesis Lectures on Data Management
Print 2153-5418   Electronic 2153-5426

Web Page Recommendation Models

Theory and Algorithms

Synthesis Lectures on Data Management

Editor

M. Tamer Özsu, *University of Waterloo*

Synthesis Lectures on Data Management is edited by Tamer Özsu of the University of Waterloo. The series will publish 50- to 125 page publications on topics pertaining to data management. The scope will largely follow the purview of premier information and computer science conferences, such as ACM SIGMOD, VLDB, ICDE, PODS, ICDT, and ACM KDD. Potential topics include, but not are limited to: query languages, database system architectures, transaction management, data warehousing, XML and databases, data stream systems, wide scale data distribution, multimedia data management, data mining, and related subjects.

Web Page Recommendation Models: Theory and Algorithms
Şule Gündüz-Ögüdücü
2010

Multidimensional Databases and Data Warehousing
Christian S. Jensen, Torben Bach Pedersen, Christian Thomsen
2010

Database Replication
Bettina Kemme, Ricardo Jimenez Peris, Marta Patino-Martinez
2010

Relational and XML Data Exchange
Marcelo Arenas, Pablo Barcelo, Leonid Libkin, Filip Murlak
2010

User-Centered Data Management
Tiziana Catarci, Alan Dix, Stephen Kimani, Giuseppe Santucci
2010

Data Stream Management
Lukasz Golab, M. Tamer Özsu
2010

Access Control in Data Management Systems
Elena Ferrari
2010

An Introduction to Duplicate Detection
Felix Naumann, Melanie Herschel
2010

Privacy-Preserving Data Publishing: An Overview
Raymond Chi-Wing Wong, Ada Wai-Chee Fu
2010

Keyword Search in Databases
Jeffrey Xu Yu, Lu Qin, Lijun Chang
2009

Web Page
Recommendation Models

Theory and Algorithms

Şule Gündüz-Ögüdücü
Istanbul Technical University

SYNTHESIS LECTURES ON DATA MANAGEMENT #10

ABSTRACT

One of the application areas of data mining is the *World Wide Web* (WWW or Web), which serves as a huge, widely distributed, global information service for every kind of information such as news, advertisements, consumer information, financial management, education, government, e-commerce, health services, and many other information services. The Web also contains a rich and dynamic collection of hyperlink information, Web page access and usage information, providing sources for data mining. The amount of information on the Web is growing rapidly, as well as the number of Web sites and Web pages per Web site. Consequently, it has become more difficult to find relevant and useful information for Web users. Web usage mining is concerned with guiding the Web users to discover useful knowledge and supporting them for decision-making. In that context, predicting the needs of a Web user as she visits Web sites has gained importance. The requirement for predicting user needs in order to guide the user in a Web site and improve the usability of the Web site can be addressed by recommending pages to the user that are related to the interest of the user at that time. This monograph gives an overview of the research in the area of discovering and modeling the users' interest in order to recommend related Web pages. The Web page recommender systems studied in this monograph are categorized according to the data mining algorithms they use for recommendation.

KEYWORDS

Web page recommendation, Web structure mining, Web content mining, Web log mining, semantic Web mining, Web log data cleaning, Web log data preparation, collaborative filtering, pattern extraction, evaluation methods

Contents

1 Introduction to Web Page Recommender Systems 1

2 Preprocessing for Web Page Recommender Models 9

    2.1   Data Collection 10

    2.2   Data Preprocessing 11

    2.3   Web Usage Data Preprocessing 12

        2.3.1 User and Session Identification 13

        2.3.2 Page Time Calculation 19

    2.4   Web Content and Structure Data Preprocessing 20

    2.5   Data Model 22

3 Pattern Extraction 27

    3.1   Collaborative Filtering 27

        3.1.1 Learning User Preferences 29

    3.2   Association Rules 35

    3.3   Clustering 38

        3.3.1 Page Clusters 38

        3.3.2 Session Clusters 43

    3.4   Sequential Patterns 45

    3.5   Combination of Web Page Recommender Systems 55

        3.5.1 Combination Methods 57

    3.6   Semantic Web 60

4 Evaluation Metrics 65

Bibliography 69

Author's Biography 77

CHAPTER 1

Introduction to Web Page Recommender Systems

This monograph starts with a gentle introduction to Web page recommender systems and their history. Readers who are familiar with these systems may skip directly to Chapter 2, where the data preprocessing steps and the data model for Web page recommender systems are introduced.

Goldberg et al. are the first developers of a recommender system, Tapestry [Goldberg et al., 1992], and they used the term "collaborative filtering" for recommender systems. However, Resnick and Varian prefer the more general term "recommender systems", because these systems may not explicitly collaborate with recipients [Resnick and Varian, 1997]. They define a typical recommender system as a system which accepts recommendations from people as inputs, aggregates them and directs them to appropriate recipients as recommendations. Furthermore, recommender systems may suggest particularly interesting items in addition to filtering undesired objects. Today, recommender systems are familiar to anyone who surfs through Web sites on Internet. There are many examples of recommender systems for commercial Web sites such as Amazon and CDNow and movie recommendation sites such as Moviefinder, Movielens or Netflix. The Alexa package (http://www.alexa.com) has a kind of recommender system for the Web, in the form of "related sites". In general, recommender systems aim to increase customer retention and loyalty on e-commerce Web sites, convert browsers into buyers, increase cross-sell by recommending related items to the active user, and help users find relevant information on a large Web site. The focus of this monograph is to study recommender systems that can be used for predicting the Web pages that are likely to be visited next in a large Web site in order to guide Web users to find information relevant to their needs. This type of recommender systems are called Web page recommender systems in this study.

Web page recommender systems are usually implemented on Web servers and make use of data obtained as a results of the collection of Web browsing patterns (implicit data) or user registration data (explicit data). The implicit approach is studied in this monograph since the user registration data are not collected in most Web sites, or it may be incomplete or unreliable even if collected. Most of the models that use implicitly gathered information are based on data mining techniques, which attempt to discover patterns or trends from a variety of data sources. Web mining is an obvious and popular one of these techniques. Web mining is defined as the use of data mining techniques to automatically discover and extract information from Web documents and services [Etzioni, 1996]. In general, Web mining is categorized into three research fields that are concerned with mining different parts of the Web: *Web Structure Mining*, *Web Content Mining* and *Web Usage Mining* [Borges and Levene,

1999; Madria et al., 1999]. While Web content and structure mining utilize real or primary data on the Web, Web usage mining, also known as Web log mining, works on the secondary data such as Web server access logs, proxy server logs, browser logs, user profiles, registration data, user sessions, cookies, user queries, and bookmark data. Web content mining usually deals with analyzing the text and multimedia content of Web pages. It discovers the valuable information from Web pages. Web structure mining deals with modeling the Web in terms of linking properties of Web pages. The Web pages can then be categorized based on their pair-wise similarities obtained from link structure. Building Web communities is one of the applications of Web structure mining [Hou and Zhang, 2002, 2003; Kleinberg, 1999]. Web usage mining refers to the application of data mining techniques to discover usage patterns from the secondary data such as Web logs, in order to understand and better serve the needs of Web-based applications. It focuses on techniques to reveal the underlying access patterns of users while interacting with the Web site.

There are two more approaches to categorize Web mining. In one approach, Web structures is treated as a part of Web contents so that Web mining can be classified simply into two categories: Web content mining and Web usage mining [Han and Kamber, 2006]. In the other approach, Web usage is included in Web structure and thus, Web mining is roughly divided into two domains: Web content mining and Web structure mining [Jicheng et al., 1999]. Although each of the three research fields of Web mining focuses on mining different objects of the Web as shown in Figure 1.1, Web page recommender models combine techniques from all the three fields. Traditional methods for recommendation are based on Web content and Web usage mining techniques. The usage data collected at different sources will represent the navigation patterns of different segments of the overall Web traffic.

Given a user's current actions, the goal of a Web page recommender system is to determine which Web pages will be accessed next. With the rapid growth of the Web, the study of modeling and predicting a user's access on a Web site has become more important. The advent of Web has caused a dramatic increase of the use of Internet as a huge, widely distributed, global information service for every kind of information. Since there is no central system to control the Web, it is impossible to estimate the precise number of Web sites and Web pages on Internet. Monthly surveys by sites like Netcraft[1] have shown that in September 2010 there are nearly 227,225,642 sites on the Web. There are numerous estimates for the number of Web pages per Web site. Thus, it becomes more important to find the useful information from these huge amounts of data. Search engines help people navigate the Internet and find the relevant Web site. Once users find the relevant Web site they need to further navigate within the site to find useful information. During the process of navigation users often experience problems, causing them to be unsure how to proceed to satisfy their original goal. As an illustration of searching a large Web site, suppose the structure of a Web site to be as in Figure 1.2. The index pages provide links to guide users to the content pages on the Web site. Even in a

---

[1] http://news.netcraft.com/archives/category/web-server-survey/, Accessed on 27 Sept. 2010.

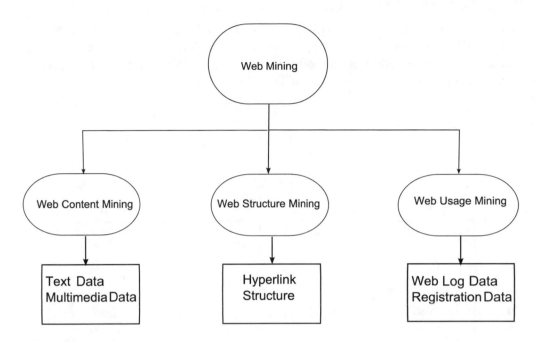

Figure 1.1: Taxonomy of Web mining

reasonably designed Web site, a user should traverse at least h Web pages to reach a content page j at depth h. The cost c_j of finding a content page j at depth h is [Aldous, 2001]:

$$c_j = \sum_{k=0}^{h-1}(1 + \frac{d(i_k)}{\gamma}) \qquad (1.1)$$

where $i_0(Home\ Page)$, $i_1, \ldots, i_{h-1}$ is the sequences of index pages to be traversed to reach content page j, $d(i)$ is the number of links at index page i and γ is the parameter reflecting the preference of the Web site designer for the average number of links on an index page. In such an environment, it becomes more important to predict the user's interest early on when the user accesses the Web site. If a Web site does not help its users satisfy their needs, they are likely to leave the site and keep surfing the Web. Although many large Web sites also offer searching via keywords, a recommender system will improve the performance of the site, and in turn, the ability of competition. This has led to the popularity of Web page recommender systems, which provide advice to users about Web pages which may contain the information they seek. It has also been used to improve the Web performance through caching, prefetching and restructuring the Web site, to recommend related pages and predicting the correct Web advertisement for users. It is important to note that the aim of this book is to study Web page recommender systems rather then Web customization systems. In customization, the structure and the content of the Web page can be tailored according to users' preferences. The users' preferences can be collected via persistent cookies, or users can save their preference settings for future customized Web site visits. However, with many users and Web pages the aim of the Web page recommender models is to recommend Web pages dynamically that contain a portion of the information content that the Web site provides.

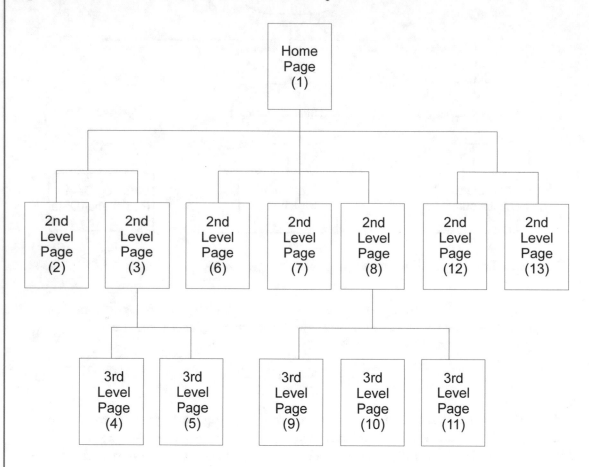

Figure 1.2: A Web site with 13 content pages and 6 index pages (horizontal lines)

Following the traditional data mining process, the overall recommendation process consists of three stages: (1) data collection and preprocessing, (2) pattern discovery and analysis, (3) recommendation (Fig. 1.3). The first two steps are conducted off-line whereas the last step is carried out on-line. The data used in a recommender system can be obtained from several sources. The main data source is Web server logs where the browsing history of users are recorded. However, the server logs should be cleaned in order to extract useful information. This task includes the removal of uninteresting data (e.g., access from Web spiders), identification of unique users and determination of user or server sessions. The term *user session* is defined as the click stream of page views for a single visit of a user to a Web site [Srivastava et al., 2000]. The extracted user sessions can be enriched using content information of Web pages or user data if available. The information provided by the data sources can all be used to construct/identify several data abstractions, such as users, server sessions, episodes, click stream, and page views [Kosala and Blockeel, 2000]. Brief surveys of the field can be found in [Chakrabarti, 2000; Kosala and Blockeel, 2000; Sebastiani, 2002; Srivastava et al., 2000]. The data prepared in this step should provide a structure to the pattern discovery and analysis step of the recommendation process. For this reason, the data model of Web page recommender systems may differ according to the technique applied in the second step. The data collection and preprocessing step will be explained in Chapter 2.

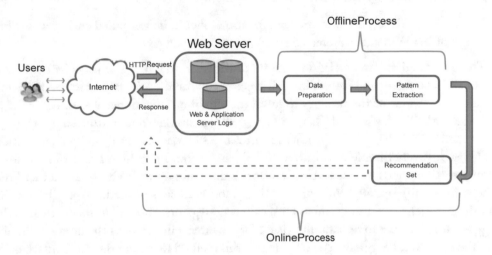

Figure 1.3: Methodology of recommender systems which perform implicit user modeling based on Web log mining techniques

Usually data mining methods are employed to automatically analyze usage patterns and generate recommendations. The main techniques used in the pattern discovery and analysis step are Collaborative Filtering (CF), clustering user sessions, association rule generation, sequential pattern generation and Markov models. Recently, hybrid methods, which combine multiple techniques to improve recommendation accuracy, have been developed. Currently, the Web is still in evolution and different approaches are being explored to add semantics to Web resources. The semantic Web enables knowledge to be processed in a way that can be used by computers not only for display purposes, but also for interoperability and integration between systems and applications. The main objective of semantic Web is to make possible the processing of Web information by computers through deploying ontologies, semantic annotation of Web content and reasoning. Semantic Web may provide an opportunity to enrich the features of a recommender system. These methods applied in the second step of the recommendation process will be introduced in Chapter 3.

The last step, the recommendation step, is the online component of a recommender system. In this step, the Web server should keep track of the active user session. The recommendation model generates recommendations as a set of links after each request of the active user. The generated recommendations can be presented to the user by adding links in the last requested Web page before the page is sent to the client browser. There are two important points to be considered in this step:

1. The method that transfers the generated recommendation set to the Web site should be compatible with the technology of the Web site. For this reason, this method should be as general as possible. For example, the need for a specific Web server, an application server, a certain programming language or a specific application developed for this purpose would decrease the usability of the recommender system.

2. The content of the presented recommendations should be formatted such that the original design of the Web site is protected from destructive changes.

The generated recommendations can be provided to the Web site users by organizing the links in HTML standard and embedding this piece of code on the Web page. However, this method is problematic in terms of the inability to fulfill the conditions mentioned above. An inline frame, which is used in HTML standard [Raggett et al., 1999] to display content from another page, is not recommended in Web design and also not supported in XHTML standard [Altheim and McCarron, 2001]. Instead, Really Simple Syndication (RSS)[2] and Atom Publishing Protocol standards [3] are commonly used methods in recent years to transfer the content of a Web site to another Web site. Especially, frequently updated Web sites, such as blog Web sites or media Web sites use RSS to publish their content. Software components, called aggregators, are used to follow such Web sites. RSS aggregators are able to periodically check for new items in the feeds the user is subscribed to. Most of the content management systems support this method to present their contents dynamically and get content from other sites. If the recommendations are generated by the recommendation module in RSS format, then they can be displayed as a set of links in the aggregator pane on the Web page using a content management system. Thus, the recommendation system can be integrated to any content management system that supports RSS. The details of this step are out of the scope of this book and not discussed in the following chapters.

The recommender systems described in this book are categorized according to the data mining methods they use for generating recommendation. This book provides a classification for the techniques used in Web page recommender systems and also includes a deep investigation of the theories beyond these techniques. The goal of such classification is to be able to answer questions like:

• What are the important features that a Web page recommendation model should provide?

• What are the needs of Web page recommender models?

---

[2]The current RSS specifications can be found at http://www.rssboard.org/rss-specification (Accessed September, 2010)

[3]This standard is controlled by *AtomEnabled Alliance* and the definition of this standard can be found at http://www.rfc-editor.org/rfc/rfc5023.txt (Accessed September, 2010)

- What are the different approaches used so far in Web page recommender models and which methods are suitable for what domain?

- What else can be contributed in Web page recommender models?

CHAPTER 2

Preprocessing for Web Page Recommender Models

In this chapter, the data collection and preprocessing steps of the recommendation process is discussed, and the resulting data models are also introduced. Web page recommender systems accept user models and a set of potential Web pages that can be recommended as input, and they generate a subset of these pages as output (Figure 2.1). Thus, recommender systems can be characterized by how they model users: explicitly or implicitly. In explicit user modeling, users supply their personal characteristics and evaluations of Web pages in the form of ratings. These data contribute to the user model matching, which is required in the recommendation process. The system predicts the utility of pages of an active user by matching, in real-time, the active user's preferences against similar records (nearest neighbors) obtained by the system over time from other users. This approach requires users to submit their feedback about pages as well as their personal information. However, this approach is not realistic since most users are reluctant to invest time or effort to rating pages [Aggarwal et al., 1999], making it impossible to use standard explicit user modeling for Web page recommendation.

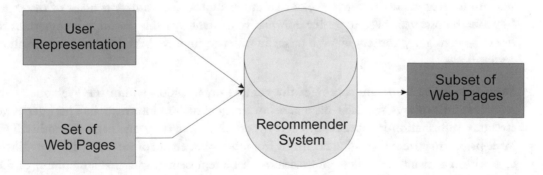

Figure 2.1: Recommendation Process

For this reason, implicit user modeling approaches are developed to minimize user collaboration. The idea is to build the user model by observation to serve as surrogates of user feedback in explicit modeling. Most of the techniques for building implicit user modeling are based on data mining. The implicit user models are formed off-line since data mining methods are complex and time consuming. A variety of information about user's preferences is obtained from several resources. User queries, the content of Web pages that a user requires during a visit, the structure of the Web site and Web log data supply valuable information about the user's interest. Web usage mining techniques are therefore often used to extract implicit user characteristics and interest.

2.1   DATA COLLECTION

The data that can be used in a Web page recommender system for a Web site is content data, structure data, user data and usage data.

- **Content Data:** The content of a Web page comprises all the objects and relationships that are visible to the users. Typically, the text content of a Web page can be represented as a feature vector containing the words that appear on the Web page and their corresponding weights. The weights can be calculated as term frequencies (TF) of the word or term frequency/inverse document frequency (TF-IDF) of the word. However, most recently Web pages contain multimedia content such as images, videos or audio files. When the aim is to recommend Web documents rather than video or images, then the multimedia files of Web pages can be easily excluded during content extraction. The site content also includes the structural meta-data, such as keywords, document attributes and predefined tags of the Web pages. However, to better understand patterns of Web site usage, the semantics of visited Web pages should be analyzed in addition to the content of these pages. The underlying domain ontology for a particular Web site can be used to further embellish the content data. Domain ontologies capture the conceptual hierarchies over Web page contents and relationships between these pages. Besides the informative primary content, Web pages also contain secondary content such as advertisements or user reviews that are related to the primary content of the page. In general, users visit Web pages for informative content. For this reason, it is important to filter the secondary content of Web pages in order to improve Web page recommendation applications.

- **Structure Data**: Structure data refer the content organization within the Web site. This organization captures the inter-page and intra-page structure information. The inter-page structure information is reflected through hyperlinks, connecting one page to another. The intra-page structure information is formed from the arrangement of various HTML or XML tags within a given page. This information can be represented as a tree structure over the space of tags extracted from the page. The structure information can be obtained by using a site mapping tool, which walks a site from the root URL, and generates a site map, which illustrates the structure of the site typically organized in hierarchical fashion.

- **User Data**: The user data that can be collected via the interaction of users and Web site depend on the Web site itself. For example, some Web sites require user registration, which typically includes a username, password, e-mail address and demographic information. Some electronic commerce Web sites collect past purchases or visit histories of users, as well as other explicit or implicit representation of users' interests such as item ratings or reviews. In this case, these data can be used to represent users' profile which allows the recommendation system to group similar users and recommend new items that similar users have liked in the past.

- **Usage Data**: The most important data source of a recommendation system is the Web server access logs collected automatically by Web and application servers. The server records the time and date of the transaction. It records the name of the file that was sent and how big that file was. It records the Internet address to which the file was sent. If the user goes to a page by clicking a link on some other page, the server records the address of the page with that link. It also records some details about how the file was sent and any errors that may have occurred as well as information about the browser that the user is using. The data recorded in the server logs reflects the (possibly concurrent) access of a Web site by multiple users. These log files can be stored in various formats such as Common log or Extended log formats. The information provided by the Web server can all be used to construct a data model consisting of several abstractions, notably, users, pages, click-streams, server sessions. In order to provide some consistency in the way these terms are defined, the World Wide Web Consortium (or W3C) has published a draft of Web term definitions relevant to analyzing Web usage. Accordingly, a Web user is a single individual who is accessing files from one or more Web servers through a Browser. A page file is the file that is served through a Hypertext Transfer Protocol (HTTP) to a user. The set of page files that contribute to a single display in a Web Browser constitutes a Web page. A Browser is a client site software application that interprets Hypertext Markup Language (HTML), the programming language of the Internet, into the words and graphics that the user sees when viewing a Web page. The click-stream is the sequence of pages followed by a user. A server session consists of a set of pages that a user requests from a single Web server during a single visit to that Web site. A session can be used as a user model for the input of the recommender model (Figure 2.1). This will be discussed in the following section in more detail.

2.2   DATA PREPROCESSING

An important task of the recommendation generation process is the creation of a preprocessed data set obtained from all available data sources. Since most of the data mining algorithms that can be applied in the next step of the recommendation process, namely the pattern discovery and analysis step, work on structured data, the aim of the preprocessing step is to form an appropriate, reliable and integrated data set that can be effectively used furhter used in the pattern discovery and analysis step. Usually, preprocessing is data-specific, and several preprocessing tasks should be performed according to the data involved in the recommendation model. For example, the preprocessing approaches that can be applied on the content data differ from the ones that can be applied on the usage data. For this reason, the preprocessing tasks applied in this step are grouped according to the data type used in the recommendation model. However, even though the data are obtained only from one data source, the preprocessing methods for this source may utilize data from other sources. For example, structure data can be employed for cleaning the usage data. Most of the work in the data preprocessing step is carried out in the preprocessing of usage data. For this reason, the preprocessing steps for usage data are explained in a separate section of this chapter. The preprocessed data sets may be fed separately to the next step or they can be integrated first. The last section of this chapter, discusses the data models that can be used in the pattern discovery and analysis step.

2.3   WEB USAGE DATA PREPROCESSING

Today's Web sites are required to host many dynamic Web pages with media content rather than static HTML Web pages. For effectiveness, the content served to the users is distributed among multiple Web or application server. With each Web server having its own log file, it is first necessary to synchronize data from multiple server logs. If cookies or user log-in information are absent, various heuristic methods (see below) can be used in this data fusion process to identify individual users in different logs. Once the log files from different Web servers are merged into one log file, this log file is passed through a preprocessing stage, which aims to reformat the original Web logs in order to identify all user sessions.

Web server logs are the primary source of usage data in which the activities of Web users are registered. These log files can be stored in various formats such as Common log or Extended log formats. Basically, an entry in Common log format consists of (1) the user's IP address, (2) the access date and time, (3) the request method (GET, POST ...), (4) the URL of the page accessed, (5) the protocol (HTTP 1.0, HTTP 1.1,...), (6) the return code, and (7) the number of bytes transmitted. A few lines of a typical access log in the Common log format for a sample Web site are presented in Table 2.1. An Extended log format file is a variant of the Common log format file that simply adds two extra fields to the end of the line, the referrer and the user agent fields.

In order to understand the user behavior the following information could be extracted from server logs:

- *Who is visiting the Web site?* One of the major steps in Web usage mining is to identify unique users in order to obtain the path that each follows.

- *The path users take through the Web pages.* With knowledge of each page that a user viewed and the order, one can identify how users navigate through the Web pages.

- *How much time users spend on each page?* A pattern of lengthy viewing time on a page might lead one to deduce that the page is interesting.

- *Where visitors are leaving the Web site?* The last page a user viewed before leaving the Web site might be a logical place to end a server session.

Web log data preprocessing converts the Web log file into the data models required for a formalized representation of the answers to these questions through extracting, decomposing, combining and deleting raw data. The first step, which is the most time consuming step of recommendation

Source of Request	User ID	Date and Time of Request	Method,URL, (HTTP Protocol)	Status Code	Num. of Bytes
		Table 2.1: Sample server logs in Common Log Format			
216.35.116.28	-	[11/Jan/2009:00:58:25 -0500]	"GET / HTTP/1.1"	200	6557
216.35.116.28	-	[11/Jan/2009:00:58:53 -0500]	"GET a.gif HTTP/1.1"	200	5478
216.35.116.28	-	[11/Jan/2009:00:59:53 -0500]	"GET b.gif HTTP/1.1"	200	6057
216.35.116.28	-	[11/Jan/2009:00:59:54 -0500]	"GET B.html HTTP/1.1"	200	59825
216.35.116.28	-	[11/Jan/2009:00:59:54 -0500]	"GET B.gif HTTP/1.1"	200	2050
24.102.227.6	-	[11/Jan/2009:00:59:55 -0500]	"GET index.html HTTP/1.1"	200	6557
216.35.116.28	-	[11/Jan/2009:00:59:55 -0500]	"GET C.html HTTP/1.1"	200	2560
24.102.227.6	-	[11/Jan/2009:00:59:56 -0500]	"GET a.gif HTTP/1.1"	200	5478
24.102.227.6	-	[11/Jan/2009:00:59:56 -0500]	"GET b.gif HTTP/1.1"	200	6057
24.102.227.6	-	[11/Jan/2009:00:59:57 -0500]	"GET D.HTML HTTP/1.1"	200	12800
24.102.227.6	-	[11/Jan/2009:00:59:58 -0500]	"GET G.gif HTTP/1.1"	200	1500
24.102.227.6	-	[11/Jan/2009:00:59:58 -0500]	"GET e.gif HTTP/1.1"	200	1230
24.102.227.6	-	[11/Jan/2009:00:59:59 -0500]	"GET e.jpg HTTP/1.1"	200	3345
216.35.116.28	-	[11/Jan/2009:00:59:59 -0500]	"GET c.jpg HTTP/1.1"	200	2247
216.35.116.28	-	[11/Jan/2009:01:00:00 -0500]	"GET E.jpg HTTP/1.1"	200	2247
216.35.116.28	-	[11/Jan/2009:01:00:00 -0500]	"GET D.html HTTP/1.1"	200	32768
216.35.116.28	-	[11/Jan/2009:01:00:01 -0500]	"GET D.gif HTTP/1.1"	200	7977
216.35.116.28	-	[11/Jan/2009:01:00:01 -0500]	"GET d.jpg HTTP/1.1"	200	6121
216.35.116.28	-	[11/Jan/2009:01:00:02 -0500]	"GET e.jpg HTTP/1.1"	200	3567
24.102.227.6	-	[11/Jan/2009:01:00:02 -0500]	"GET C.html HTTP/1.1"	200	32768
24.102.227.6	-	[11/Jan/2009:08:57:02 -0500]	"GET / HTTP/1.1"	200	32768
24.102.227.6	-	[11/Jan/2009:08:58:53 -0500]	"GET a.gif HTTP/1.1"	200	5478
24.102.227.6	-	[11/Jan/2009:08:59:53 -0500]	"GET b.gif HTTP/1.1"	200	6057
24.102.227.6	-	[11/Jan/2009:09:01:00 -0500]	"GET D.html HTTP/1.1"	200	32768
24.102.227.6	-	[11/Jan/2009:09:01:45 -0500]	"GET D.gif HTTP/1.1"	200	7977
24.102.227.6	-	[11/Jan/2009:09:02:25 -0500]	"GET d.jpg HTTP/1.1"	200	6121
24.102.227.6	-	[11/Jan/2009:09:03:02 -0500]	"GET e.jpg HTTP/1.1"	200	3567

process, is to clean the data and prepare for mining the usage patterns. Fundamental methods of data cleaning and preparation have been well studied in [Cooley et al., 1999; Srivastava et al., 2000; Zaïane, 2001]. A brief discussion is provided in the following subsections.

2.3.1 USER AND SESSION IDENTIFICATION

In order to extract user behavior, each request in the log file should be uniquely assigned to the individual that has performed it. It is an easy task if the log file contains a person ID such as login to the server or to the user's own computer. However, most Web sites do not require users to log in, and most Web servers do not make a request to learn the user's login identity on her own computer. Thus, the information available according to the HTTP standard is not adequate to distinguish among users from the same host or proxy. More often, it is an IP address assigned by an Internet Service

Provider (ISP) or corporate proxy server to a user's TCP/IP connection to the site, preventing unique identification.

The most widespread remedy for this problem is the use of cookies. A cookie is a small piece of code associated with a Web site; it installs itself in the user's host and associates a cookie identifier with user's browser. The contents of a cookie file depend on the Web site being visited and on the browser. In general, a cookie has at least the following six fields: (1) name-value, (2) domain, (3) path, (4) expires, and (5) secure. The name-value pair is a compulsory field which specifies the name of the cookie, by which it can be referenced later. It contains the actual data that the cookie is going to store. The remaining fields are optional. The domain field specifies the domain portion of the URLs for which the cookie is valid. The path field specifies the directory where the cookie is active. The expires field is used to set the expiry date of the cookie, after which, the cookie will no longer be stored by the client or sent to the server. If the secure field is specified, a cookie is sent to HTTP servers using SSL (Secure Sockets Layer) protocol known as HTTPS servers. If this attribute is not specified, the cookie will be sent over any channel, involving an unsecured one also. The Web site stores these data on user's machine, and later, it receives it back. A Web site can only use its own cookie file on the user's machine. If a user accesses a Web site, the user's browser will look on a user's machine for a cookie file that the Web site has previously sent. If it finds a cookie file for the Web site, it will send all of the name-value pairs in the cookie file to the Web site's server along with the URL. If it doen't find a cookie file, it will not send cookie data. If a user accesses a Web site for the first time, there will be no cookie file returned for that domain because the cookie hasn't been created yet. The Web server creates a new ID for the user in the Web site's database and then sends name-value pairs to the user's machine in the header for the Web page it sends. The header of the Web page is the content(s) that exist between the <head> HTML tag. This content is not viewable from the user's standpoint (except for the title, which is evident in the page's title).

Another way of identifying unique users is using a heuristic method, which identifies an unique IP address as an user, bearing in mind that a single IP can be used by a group of users. In cases when IP addresses resolve into domain names registered to a person or company, it is possible to gather more specific information.

Both methods have certain disadvantages. The user identification method based on cookies may suffer when the user turns off the cookie support in the browser. Another problem of this method may occur when the user deletes the cookie files located in the local machine. When this individual revisits the Web site, the user is regarded as a new user. The other possibility is that the same computer may be used by different users. A problem that may occur when identifying users by IP addresses is that the same IP address may be used by a group of users. The choice of the particular method should be dependent on the characteristics of the data at hand.

The page requests made by the automated agents and spider programs traversing links can often cause a skewed analysis. The simplest method for dealing with agent traffic is to check the agent field of the usage data. A simple string match during the data cleaning step can remove a significant amount of agent traffic. Robots that follow the conventions outlined in the Robot Exclusion Protocol, which has been proposed to provide advisory regulations for robots [Koster, 1996], will check for the existence of a file named "robot.txt". An agent can be identified through the agent field or by the requesting "robot.txt" file. The log entries that are made by an agent are removed from the log data. The aforementioned steps eventually produce a set of users $\mathcal{U} = \{u_1, ..., u_K\}$ with unique user IDs $(1 \ldots K)$ who have been visiting the Web site between the time period of the server log files.

Once the users are identified, server log data passes through a session reconstruction step. The process of reconstructing the users' original sessions by using server log data is defined as session reconstruction. However, before constructing user sessions, the URLs in the log file should be normalized in order to determine same Web pages, which are represented by syntactically different URLs. This can be done by extracting the content of Web pages. The content, structure and semantic information of Web pages can be obtained using a Web crawler. A Web crawler accesses the selected Web site, to which a recommender model will be built, using the HTTP/1.1 protocol defined by the W3C. Examples of some open source Web crawlers are Heritrix[1], JoBo[2], JSpider[3], Metis[4], and WebSphinx[5]. Using an appropriate Web crawler the content and the meta-data of each page on the Web site can be obtained as well as the structure of the Web site. According to the needs of the recommender model, a Web page p_i can be represented by a set of weighted terms found in the textual content (or meta-data) and links pointing to other pages in the same Web site. A common form for each page is chosen using a Web crawler. Only links that point to the Web pages within the site are added to the list of pages to explore. Comparing the content of pages provides a way to determine different URLs belonging to the same Web page. In this phase, a set of pages of the Web site $\mathcal{P} = \{p_1, ..., p_N\}$ is obtained. Table 2.2 shows the extracted pages assigned to the HTML pages in the sample log data in Table 2.1. The HTML pages and their mapped page numbers are termed as "URL" and "Page" in the Table.

Table 2.2: Set of pages for sample log data.

URL	Page
index.html	p_1
B.html	p_2
C.html	p_3
D.html	p_4

[1] http://crawler.archive.org/, Accessed July, 2010.
[2] http://www.matuschek.net/software/jobo/, Accessed July, 2010.
[3] http://sourceforge.net/projects/j-spider/, Accessed July, 2010.
[4] http://www.severus.org/sacha/metis/, Accessed July, 2010.
[5] http://www.cs.cmu.edu/~rcm/websphinx/, Accessed July, 2010.

Reconstructing user sessions from server logs is a challenging task since the access log protocol is stateless and connectionless. If neither the cookie nor the user-login information are available, the reconstruction of original sessions is based on two basic heuristics: (1) time oriented (h1, h2) and (2) navigation oriented (h3).

Table 2.3: User sessions for the sample log data using h2 heuristic. Each unique IP address is assigned to an individual user and the duration of a user session is set to 30 minutes.

UID	Date-Time	File	Page	SID
	[11/Jan/2009:00:58:25 -0500]	/	p_1	
	[11/Jan/2009:00:58:53 -0500]	a.gif		
	[11/Jan/2009:00:58:53 -0500]	b.gif		
	[11/Jan/2009:00:59:54 -0500]	**B.html**	p_2	
	[11/Jan/2009:00:59:54 -0500]	B.gif		
1	**[11/Jan/2009:00:59:55 -0500]**	**C.html**	p_3	1
	[11/Jan/2009:00:59:59 -0500]	c.jpg		
	[11/Jan/2009:01:00:00 -0500]	E.jpg		
	[11/Jan/2009:01:00:00 -0500]	**D.html**	p_4	
	[11/Jan/2009:01:00:01 -0500]	D.gif		
	[11/Jan/2009:01:00:01 -0500]	d.jpg		
	[11/Jan/2009:01:00:02 -0500]	e.jpg		
	[11/Jan/2009:00:59:55 -0500]	**index.html**	p_1	
	[11/Jan/2009:00:59:56 -0500]	a.gif		
	[11/Jan/2009:00:59:56 -0500]	b.gif		
	[11/Jan/2009:00:59:57 -0500]	**D.html**	p_4	
2	[11/Jan/2009:00:59:58 -0500]	G.gif		2
	[11/Jan/2009:00:59:58 -0500]	e.gif		
	[11/Jan/2009:00:59:59 -0500]	e.jpg		
	[11/Jan/2009:01:00:02 -0500]	**C.html**	p_3	
	[11/Jan/2009:08:57:02 -0500]	/	p_1	
	[11/Jan/2009:08:58:53 -0500]	a.gif		
	[11/Jan/2009:08:59:53 -0500]	b.gif		
2	**[11/Jan/2009:09:01:00 -0500]**	**D.html**	p_4	3
	[11/Jan/2009:09:01:45 -0500]	D.gif		
	[11/Jan/2009:09:02:25 -0500]	d.jpg		
	[11/Jan/2009:09:03:02 -0500]	e.jpg		

The time oriented heuristic relies on total session time or page visiting time. In the first type ($h1$), the duration of a session must not exceed a given threshold. In the second type ($h2$), the time spent on a page must not exceed a given threshold. A new session is created when a new user is encountered, if the time difference between two consecutive page requests, or if the time spent in the same session exceeds a predefined threshold for the same user. Commonly used time thresholds for h1 and h2 are 30 and 10 minutes, respectively. It was found that a 25.5 minute cutoff time for session duration can be used [Catledge and Pitkow, 1995]. In many commercial products this timeout has been rounded up to 30 minutes. A 10-minute threshold for page-stay time is proposed in [Spiliopoulou et al., 2003]. However, different Web site structures may have different thresholds for h1 and h2. Table 2.3 presents the user sessions for individual users extracted from sample log data in Table 2.1 where the HTML pages are written as bold. The users are identified by the IP addresses in the log, and a unique number is associated to each user (UID in the Table 2.3). The h2 heuristic is employed for the session identification, and similarly, a unique number is assigned to each session of a user (SID in the Table 2.3).

The navigation oriented heuristic ($h3$) considers the site topology. Accesses to cached pages are not recorded in the Web log due to the browser or proxy cache. Therefore, references to those pages are missed. The missing references in the log file can be found using a set of assumptions. The referrer field of the Web log or the Web site structure can be used to infer cached pages. If a requested Web page p_i is not reachable from previously visited pages in a session, then a new session is constructed starting with page p_i.

Algorithm 1 Construction of user sessions from Web server logs using $h1$ heuristic

---

Input : Web server logs
Output : set of user sessions $\mathcal{S} = \{s_1, ..., s_M\}$

1: $\mathcal{S} = \{\emptyset\}$
2: Order all Web logs by user IDs (u_k) and time increasingly
3: **for all** user ID u_k **do**
4:      Create a new user session in $\mathcal{S}$ for user u_k
5:      **for** i=1 to the number of records of this u_k **do**
6:          **if** $t_{i+1} - t_i < \triangle t$ **then**
7:              insert this record into user session
8:          **else**
9:              Create a new user session in $\mathcal{S}$ for user u_k
10:         **end if**
11:     **end for**
12: **end for**

The irrelevant page requests, which comprise of URLs of embedded objects, with filename suffixes such as, gif, jpeg, GIF, JPEG, jpg, JPG can be removed from user sessions. Eventually, this step produces a set of user sessions $\mathcal{S} = \{s_1, ..., s_M\}$. Algorithm 1 presents the algorithm for the session identification when an $h1$ type heuristic is applied. In this algorithm, t_i is the timestamp of the ith record belonging to a user in the server logs. A user session s_m is a sequence of activities performed by a user u_k when navigating through a given site. Short user sessions can be removed in order to eliminate random accesses to the Web site [Mobasher et al., 2001c, 2002]. Table 2.4 shows the extracted user sessions where non-HTML log entries in user sessions in Table 2.3 are removed. The remaining pages are represented as in Table 2.2.

Table 2.4: User sessions mapped to the set of pages. h2 heuristic is used.		
UID	SID	User Session
1	1	p_1, p_2, p_3, p_4
2	2	p_1, p_4, p_3
2	3	p_1, p_4

After user and session identification, the missing pages in user access paths, due to the Browser or proxy servers caching, can be appended by using the referrer-based method. This process is called as path completion. When using path completion, the first session of user 1 is reconstructed as in Fig. 2.2. In this figure, the site structure is given where the solid arrows show the hyperlinks. The dashed arrows show the actual path the user takes in the site where the first page request is p_1. After reaching page p_3 from p_2, the user has returned back to page p_2. The second request for page p_2 has been not recorded in the Web server logs since it is served by the cache of the user's browser. Thus, the log records show that the user requested page p_4 after visiting page p_3.

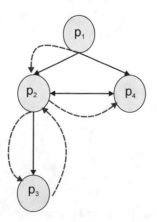

Session 1 of user 1 extracted from server log:

$p_1 \rightarrow p_2 \rightarrow p_3 \rightarrow p_4$

Actual navigation path of the user based on h3 heuristic:

$p_1 \rightarrow p_2 \rightarrow p_3 \rightarrow p_2 \rightarrow p_4$

Figure 2.2: Missing references due to the caching

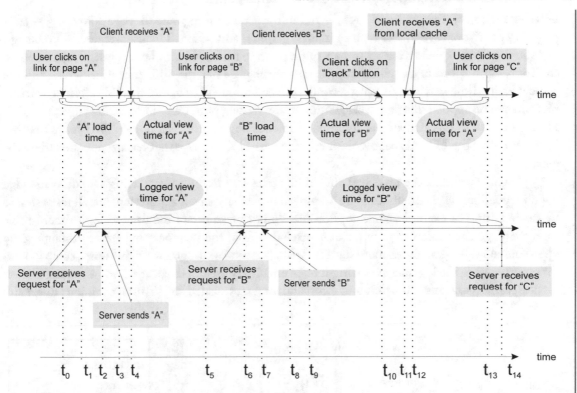

Figure 2.3: Timeline for page file request and response

2.3.2   PAGE TIME CALCULATION

In order to assess the interest of a visitor to a Web page, the visiting page time for each page, which is defined as the time difference between consecutive page requests for the user in the same session, can be calculated. For the last page of the user session, the visiting page time is the mean of the times for that page taken across all sessions in which it is not the last page request. This measurement is subject to a fair amount of noise as the user's behavior can not always be accurately determined, e.g., the user could be getting a cup of coffee, talking on the phone or accurately reading the page. However, it is assumed that such interruptions while visiting a Web page are in the minority. Since it is impossible to determine the accurate behavior of a Web user, these interruptions could appear as outliers in the data set. With a sufficiently large data set the common behavior of Web users in terms of visiting page times could be determined in spite of these outliers. However, if the size of the data set is insufficient for determining the common behavior of Web users, the prediction accuracy of the recommendation model could be low.

Another problem is that the visiting time of a page recorded in a server log is often longer than the actual visiting time on the client side. As shown in Figure 2.3 [Cooley et al., 1999], the time between requests for pages A and B is $t_6 - t_1$, but the actual visiting time for page A is only $t_5 - t_4$. A page can consist of several files such as frames, graphics and scripts. The user requests a Web page, but she does not explicitly ask for frames or graphics to be loaded into her browser. Depending on the connection speed of the client and the size of the page file, the difference in recorded, and the actual visiting time may range from a second to several minutes. To reduce this side effect, a heuristic method can be applied during the calculation of the visiting page time. The visiting page time of an HTML page can be calculated as the time difference between the last non-HTML page that has been sent after the HTML page request and the next HTML page that has been requested by the user.

Fig. 2.4 presents the tasks that should be performed in the preprocessing step of Web usage data. Depending on the methods to be employed in the pattern extraction step, not all tasks should be carried out. For example, some applications do not make use of the page visiting time. In this case, the page time calculation task can be excluded from the preprocessing step. Although some open source Web log analyzer tools, such as Analog[6] Awstats[7], Logminer[8], Polliwog[9], can be found for preprocessing the log data, preparing it to be effectively used in the next step of recommendation process, which consumes 80% to 90% of effort and resources needed for Web usage mining [Edelstein, March 2001].

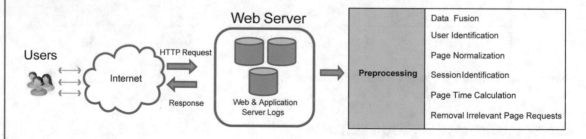

Figure 2.4: Preprocessing tasks for Web usage data

2.4 WEB CONTENT AND STRUCTURE DATA PREPROCESSING

Some of the recommendation models make use of the content data as a secondary data source. The main idea of these kinds of recommendation models is that if a user is interested in a Web page p_i then she is likely to be interested in a "similar" page. Similarity between Web pages can be calculated based on the information on these pages. Besides, the information on a browsed Web page is a good

---

[6]http://www.analog.cx/, Accessed July, 2010.
[7]http://awstats.sourceforge.net/, Accessed July, 2010.
[8]http://logminer.sourceforge.net/, Accessed July, 2010.
[9]http://polliwog.sourceforge.net/, Accessed July, 2010.

indicator of user interest. The information on a Web page can be represented both by the text content and the meta data, such as title and keywords, of these pages. In order to make better use of the information on Web page, first the "noise content" should be eliminated. There are two groups of noise content: global noise and local noise [Zhang et al., 2004]. On a Web site, global noise is caused by duplicated Web pages and near- replicas whereas local noises is caused by irrelevant content on a Web page such as advertisements, navigation panels, and copyright announcements, etc. Global noise not only leads to a large waste of disk space storing the duplicated pages, but also, and more important for a Web page recommender system, to a decrease in the accuracy of recommender systems in terms of generating correct recommendations. Local noise makes it difficult to extract the content of a Web page, so it also decreases the accuracy of the Web page recommender system. Thus, before utilizing the content of Web pages for building users' preference model, a preprocessing stage for Web content data becomes inevitable.

To eliminate global noise, one of the well-known approaches, used also by search engines to detect near-replica Web pages, can be employed [Shivakumar and Garcia-Molina, 1998]. These approaches are based on the computing of a set of fingerprints for each page. If the amount of identical fingerprints in two pages reaches a threshold, the two pages are considered as a pair of replicas. At the end of this stage, the number of Web pages in the set $\mathcal{P}$ may decrease.

The approaches for removing local noise from Web pages make use of Web content mining techniques [Wang et al., 2007; Xiaoli and Zhongzhi, 2002]. The Web pages can be first described by using HTML tags. In HTML, there are different text fields, such as *title*, *meta-data* and *body*. The content of a Web page can be extracted by identifying these fields and extracting the text that appears between appropriate HTML tags, for example, between body tags or title tags. However, this approach may cause some problems by including texts in the content field of a Web page that should not be included. Information Extraction (IE) systems can also be used to extract the structural information from HTML pages, based on manually generated templates or examples [Hsu and Dung, 1998; Kushmerick, 1997]. Most of the Web sites generate Web pages by retrieving data from a database and inserting them into fixed templates. Since Web page recommender systems work generally on a specific Web site, the templates of the Web site in question can be used for identifying the main content block. The meta tags on a Web page are used to obtain meta data from a Web page. Thus, the Web page content can be isolated from structure data (HTML and XML tags, meta-tags, etc.).

After removing local noise, the content on Web pages can be represented in several ways. The most straightforward approach is to use Vector Space Model (VSM). In this model, a Web page is represented as a feature vector of keywords (terms) that appear in the entire set of Web pages $\mathcal{P}$ on the Web site. Each Web page can be represented as follows:

$$\overrightarrow{p}_i = \{(w_{i1}, t_1), \ldots, (w_{in}, t_r)\} \tag{2.1}$$

The features $t_1, \ldots, t_r$ are the keywords that appear in $\mathcal{P}$; w_{ij} is the weight of keyword t_j, if t_j appears in p_i and 0, otherwise. The TF or the TF-IDF weight method is often used to calculate the weights of keywords. The TF weight [Baldi et al., 2003] of a keyword t_j in the Web page p_i can be calculated with the following formula:

$$TF_{ij} = \frac{f_{ij}}{\sum_{k=1}^{r} f_{ik}} \qquad (2.2)$$

where f_{ik} is the number of times that the keyword t_k appears in Web page p_i. Inverse Document Frequency (IDF) of a keyword t_j, which measures the general "importance" of that keyword, is calculated as:

$$IDF_j = \log \frac{n_j}{N} \qquad (2.3)$$

where n_j is the number of Web pages where the jth keyword appears, and N is total number of Web pages in the set $\mathcal{P}$. Then TF-IDF weight of a keyword t_j in Web page p_i is computed as:

$$TFIDF_{ij} = TF_{ij} \times IDF_j \qquad (2.4)$$

However, some of the Web pages are not rich in content. For example, it is difficult to extract keywords from Web pages comprising images, videos, programs, etc. Furthermore, some Web pages may not include keywords that are the most descriptive ones for their content. Therefore, *anchor window*, which is defined as the information contained in the links that point to the Web page and the text near them, is used for characterizing a Web page [Chakrabarti, 2000]. The assumption behind this is that the text around the link to a page is descriptive of its contents.

The semantic or structured meta data embedded in Web pages or Web site can also be included in the Web content data. The content data can be enriched and augmented through the addition of information from domain ontology represented as concept hierarchy.

The structure data that can be used in Web page recommender system consist of the link structure of the Web site. This link structure can be obtained by using a site mapping tool, or it can be also obtained through methods comprising the stage of removing the local noise.

2.5   DATA MODEL

A Web page recommender model accepts the set of Web pages at a Web site and the representation of users as input, and it generates a subset of the Web pages as output. In general, the recommendation problem can be formulated as follows [Gediminas and Alexander, 2005]: Let $\mathcal{U} = \{u_1, ..., u_K\}$ be the set of users of the Web site obtained from registration data or from the server logs, and let $\mathcal{P} = \{p_1, ..., p_N\}$ be the set of all Web pages that can be recommended. Let $g(u_k, p_n)$ be a utility function that measures the gain or usefulness of page p_n to user u_k, i.e., $g : \mathcal{U} \times \mathcal{P} \rightarrow \mathcal{R}$ where $\mathcal{R}$ is a totally ordered set (e.g., non negative integers or real numbers within a certain range). Then, for each user $u_k \in \mathcal{U}$, the aim of a Web page recommender model is to choose a Web page $p' \in \mathcal{P}$ that maximizes the user's utility:

$$\forall u_k \in \mathcal{U}, \quad p'_{u_k} = \arg\max_{p_n \in \mathcal{P}} g(u_k, p_n) \qquad (2.5)$$

Thus, the data model for representing the users is essential and crucial for Web page recommender models. It is obvious that the data model depends highly on the available data sources and the algorithm to be used to generate the recommendation. Since data mining algorithms are usually employed on structured data, there is a tendency to convert the Web data into a structured format such as matrix expression $\mathcal{A}$. In this expression, the rows of the matrix correspond to the objects and the columns correspond to the attributes. Each cell $a(i, j)$ of the matrix is the value of the jth attribute of the ith object (Fig. 2.5).

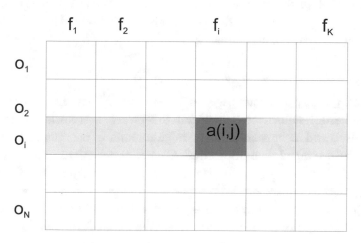

Figure 2.5: Matrix expression of Web data model

Matrix expression is widely used in many Web mining applications. The matrix expression shown in Fig. 2.5 can also be used to represent all the data collected for building a recommendation model. For example, a *page-term matrix* can be used to represent the content data. In this case, the rows and columns correspond to the Web pages and to the words appearing on the whole Web site, respectively. The matrix can be weighted binary where a 1 in a cell $a(i, j)$ denotes the presence of term t_j on page p_i. The values of each cell in this matrix could be also calculated using Eq. 2.2 or Eq. 2.4. The transpose of this matrix is *term-page matrix*. Fig. 2.6(a) shows an example for a term-page matrix with binary weighting.

Likewise, the matrix expression can be used to model the structure of the Web site. The linkage information of the Web site can be represented as an adjacency matrix, which is a non-symmetric square matrix of size N, N being the number of Web pages on the Web site. Each cell $a(i, j)$ of the matrix has a value either 1 or 0, where a value of 1 indicates that there is hyperlink from page p_i to page p_j and 0 indicates its absence. The hyperlinks are directed, i.e., the two Web pages involved in a hyperlink play different roles: one is source, the other is target. Given a hyperlink directed from source page p_i to target page p_j, the link is an out-link for p_i, while an in-link for p_j. Thus, the out-link relationships of a page p_i is represented by the ith row of the matrix where the in-link properties of that page is represented by the ith column of the matrix.

The Web user sessions can be modeled as sequence data. In general, a user session s_m of a length l is as follows:

$$s_m = \langle (p_1^m, w_{p_1^m}), (p_2^m, w_{p_2^m}), \ldots, (p_l^m, w_{p_l^m}) \rangle \tag{2.6}$$

where $p_j^i = p_n$ for some $n \in \{1, \ldots, N\}$ and $w_{p_j^m}$ is its corresponding weight representing the importance of the Web page in session s_m. When it is not necessary to preserve the users sessions as sequences for the Web page recommendation model, the Web user sessions can also be modeled using matrix expression. Then, a user sessions s_m can also be represented by an N-dimensional vector of visited pages over the space of page references:

$$\vec{s_m} = \langle w_{p_\Delta^m}, \ldots, w_{p_k^m}, \ldots, w_{p_N^m} \rangle \tag{2.7}$$

where N is the total number of unique pages in the Web site. When the number of Web pages at a Web site is huge, it becomes much more inefficient to represent user sessions in terms of Web pages. Complex data analysis and recommendation on huge amounts of data can take a long time, making such a recommendation in real time impractical. Clustering techniques can be applied to obtain a reduced representation of Web pages that is much smaller in volume. The cluster representations of Web pages are used to replace the Web pages. Each cluster can be represented by a category, and each Web page can be mapped to the category to which it belongs. Thus, a user session can be represented by these categories instead of individual Web pages. Although this method may yield a decrease in the Web page prediction accuracy, it may be necessary for sites with a huge number of Web pages.

	web	data	mining	information	extraction
p_1	0	1	1	1	1
p_2	0	1	1	0	0
p_3	1	0	1	0	0
p_4	1	1	1	1	1

(a) Term-page matrix for a sample Web site

	p_1	p_2	p_3	p_4
S_1	1	1	1	1
S_2	1	0	1	1
S_3	1	0	0	1

(b) Session-page matrix for the sample Web log data

Figure 2.6: Matrix representations of content and usage data

There are several ways to determine the weights of pages in a session. For example, the weights can be binary where a one of a weight $w_{p_j^m}$ associated with a page p_j^m represents the existence of that page in session s_m; or the weights can be (normalized) visiting time of the duration of the associated page in the user's session representing the significance of that page.

The visiting time of a page can be normalized either across the page visiting times in a single session or across the visiting times of that page in all sessions [Mobasher et al., 2001b]. The first type of normalization is performed as follows:

$$norm_p(w_{p_i^m}) = \frac{w_{p_i^m} - \min_{1 \leqslant j \leqslant N}\{w_{p_j^m}\}}{\max_{1 \leqslant j \leqslant N}\{w_{p_j^m}\} - \min_{1 \leqslant j \leqslant N}\{w_{p_j^m}\}} \tag{2.8}$$

This normalization captures the relative significance of a page within one user session with respect to other pages accessed during the same user session. The second type of normalization can be performed as follows:

$$norm_S(w_{p_i^m}) = \frac{w_{p_i^m} - \min_{s_j \in S}\{w_{p_i^j}\}}{\max_{s_j \in S}\{w_{p_i^j}\} - \min_{s_j \in S}\{w_{p_i^j}\}} \tag{2.9}$$

This type of normalization captures the relative weight of a page in a user session with respect to the weights of the same page for all other user sessions.

A *session–page matrix* A of size M and N can be constructed where M and N are the number of user sessions and the number of Web pages on the Web site, respectively. A matrix cell $a(i, j)$ is determined by the weight of page p_j in user session s_i. Fig. 2.6(b) shows a session-page matrix with binary weights for the session in Table 2.4. In this case, the ordering information in user sessions has been lost.

	web	data	mining	information	extraction
S_1	2	3	4	2	2
S_2	2	2	3	2	2
S_3	1	2	2	2	2

Figure 2.7: Session-term matrix

For an effective Web page recommender system, the data obtained from multiple sources can be integrated. This can be done just after the preprocessing steps are performed separately on each data set. One way of doing this is through the multiplication of the data matrices. For example, in order to obtain content enhanced sessions, the session-page matrix can be multiplied by the page-term matrix, resulting in a session-term matrix as illustrated in Fig. 2.7. Each row of this matrix is a user session, and each column corresponds to a keyword extracted from the Web site. Thus, the data in the session-term matrix represent the interest of user in a session in terms of semantic features of the Web page contents. Various data mining tasks can be performed on the session-term matrix to build usage patterns.

The data obtained from multiple sources can be integrated during the recommendation step by combining the results from the data mining algorithms applied on the data sets separately [Mobasher et al., 2000]. There are several methods to integrate data from multiple sources during the recommendation process such as hybrid recommender models. These methods will be explained in the next chapter in detail.

CHAPTER 3

Pattern Extraction

This section describes usage pattern discovery algorithms that have been applied in Web page recommendation. It is very difficult to classify these algorithms based on the data mining techniques they use for user modeling. In most of the methods, techniques are combined together for discovering usage patterns. Some of the works are proposed only for user modeling, and the discovered patterns are not used for recommendation. However, the discovered usage patterns in these works are appropriate to integrate them as a part of recommender systems. For this reason, they are included in this monograph. The techniques described in this chapter are categorized into broad classes, namely: (1) collaborative filtering, (2) association rules, (3) clustering, (4) sequential patterns, (5) combination of Web page recommender systems, and (6) semantic Web. All the techniques are described in terms of their applicability for usage pattern extraction in a Web page recommender system rather than their general usage in a data mining application.

3.1 COLLABORATIVE FILTERING

Goldberg et al. are the first developers of a recommender system, Tapestry [Goldberg et al., 1992], and they used the term *Collaborative Filtering* for recommender systems. The system relied on the explicit opinions of people from a small community, such as an office work group. However, recommender systems for large communities can not depend on everyone knowing each other. Later on, several ratings-based automated recommender systems were developed.

Collaborative Filtering (CF) systems collect visitor opinions on a set of objects, using ratings explicitly provided by the users or implicitly computed. In explicit rating, users assign ratings to items, or a positive (or negative) vote to some document. The implicit ratings are computed by considering, for example, the access to a Web page. A *rating matrix* is constructed where each row represents a user and each column represents an item. Items could be any type of online information resources or products in an online community such as Web pages, videos, music tracks, photos, academic papers, books, etc. CF systems predict a particular user's interest in an item using the rating matrix (Fig. 3.1). Alternatively, the item-item matrix, which contains the pair-wise similarities of items, can be used as the rating matrix. The memory based CF systems are often based on matching, in real-time, the current user's profile against similar records (nearest neighbors) obtained by the system over time from other users. Besides their low accuracy, when data are sparse, memory based CF methods suffer from a limited scalability problem for large datasets. To achieve a better performance and handle these shortcomings of memory-based CF systems, model-based approaches are proposed. The model-based CF algorithms are inspired from data mining and machine learning algorithms where a model is developed using the rating matrix to generate recommendations. Well-known model-based techniques are clustering and classification, which will be explained in the subsequent sections. Hybrid CF approaches such as content-based systems work by comparing text descriptions or other representations associated with an item. A detailed discussion of recommender systems based on CF techniques can be found in [Herlocker et al., 2004].

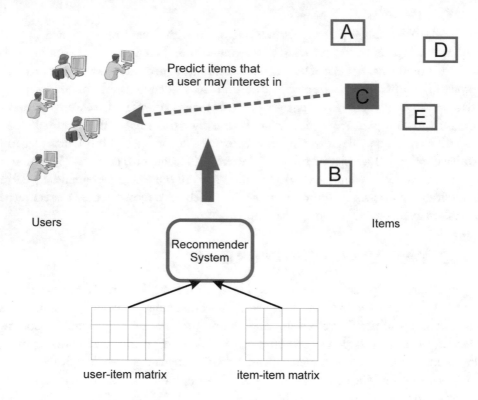

Figure 3.1: Collaborative Filtering Recommender System

Traditional CF based systems work as follows:

1. The preferences of a large group of people are registered. These preferences could be items bought by the user on a e-commerce Web site, or Web pages visited by the user.

2. According to a similarity metric, a subgroup of people are selected whose preferences are similar to the current user's preferences.

3. Using a function, such as average, the preferences of that subgroup are calculated.

4. Based on the calculated preferences, a set of items not already accessed or purchased by the active user are selected to generate a recommendation set.

Rating matrix is the basis of CF methods. The ratings collected by the system may be both implicit and explicit. Although CF techniques based on implicit rating are available for recommendation, most of the CF approaches are developed for recommending items where users can provide their preferences with explicit ratings to items. Fig. 3.2(a) and Fig. 3.2(b) show a typical CF approach for movie recommendations where the ratings are explicit. Based on these ratings, non-personalized recommendations, which are identical to each user, are generated (Fig. 3.3). It is frequently the case that ratings are made on an agreed discrete scale. These ratings allow the users' preferences to be processed statistically to provide averages, ranges, distributions, etc., which make CF approaches applicable. In Web page recommendation, ratings correspond the satisfaction of users' requirements when visiting a Web page. Since it is not useful for Web page recommender systems to collect these ratings explicitly, they may be gathered implicitly. There are not many studies that assess the impact of predictive models of user satisfaction and interest used with implicit ratings for recommender accuracy. It has been assumed that the implicit ratings can be inferred from the visiting times of Web pages or simply from visiting a page. In this section, pure CF techniques will be described, followed by an explanation of how these techniques are used in a Web page recommender system.

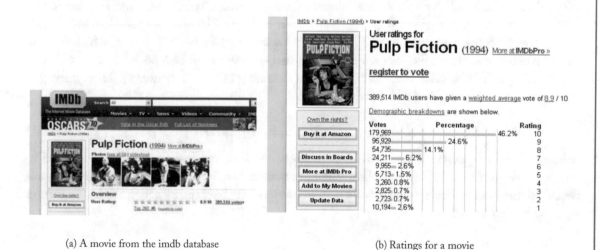

(a) A movie from the imdb database   (b) Ratings for a movie

Figure 3.2: A movie from the Internet movie database (www.imdb.com)

3.1.1   LEARNING USER PREFERENCES

The main idea of CF system is to recommend new items to users based on similarities of their preferences. This type of CF systems are called user-centric. The item-centric CF systems, by contrast, consider the similarities between items. We discuss both approaches in this section.

Figure 3.3: A sample CF system in IMDB

User Centric Collaborative Filtering: User centric CF approaches aim to find correlations among users. The similarities between users are calculated using a rating matrix. First, when recommending a set of items to an active user, called *neighbors* [Schafer et al., 2007] to the corresponding user, highly rated items by those users are found. The CF systems then make a prediction as to which of these items an active user would like. For K users and N items, a user u_i can be represented by the ith row of the rating matrix $\mathbf{X}$. Each element r_{ik} indicates the rating of item i_k by user u_i. Thus, the rating matrix $\mathbf{X}$ can be decomposed into its row vectors:

$$\mathbf{X} = [u_1, \ldots, u_K]^T, \quad u_i = [r_{i1}, \ldots, r_{iN}] \tag{3.1}$$

where each row represent a user profile in terms of the item ratings. These vectors are used to compute user similarities. Cosine similarity and Pearson's correlation are popular similarity measures for calculating similarities among users. The Cosine similarity between an active user u_x and a user u_y is calculated as follows:

$$sim_{cos}(u_x, u_y) = \sum_{j=1}^{N} \frac{r_{xj}}{\sqrt{\sum_{k=1}^{N} r_{xk}^2}} \frac{r_{yj}}{\sqrt{\sum_{k=1}^{N} r_{yk}^2}} \tag{3.2}$$

The range of Cosine similarity is [0, 1]. A value of zero indicates that the corresponding user profiles are totally different where a value of one indicates that they are totally similar.

One of the first CF systems, the GroupLens system for Usenet newsgroups [Konstan et al., 1997], defined the similarity between two users as the Pearson's correlations coefficient:

$$sim_{PC}(u_x, u_y) = \frac{\sum_{j=1}^{N} (r_{xj} - \bar{r}_x)(r_{yj} - \bar{r}_y)}{\sqrt{\sum_{k=1}^{N} (r_{xk} - \bar{r}_x)^2} \sqrt{\sum_{k=1}^{N} (r_{yk} - \bar{r}_y)^2}} \tag{3.3}$$

where $\bar{r}_i$ denotes the average rating made by user u_i. Pearson's correlation coefficient ranges between -1 and 1, indicating perfect disagreement and perfect agreement of users, respectively. The neighbors $\mathcal{S}_n(u_x)$ of an active user u_x can be identified by employing a threshold value for the similarity or by selecting top-K users. In the top-K case, the users are sorted according to their similarity values, and for K, most similar users are selected as $\mathcal{S}_n(u_x)$. Consequently, the predicted rating of an item i_k by an active user u_x is computed as [Schafer et al., 2007]:

$$\widehat{r}_{xk} = \bar{u}_x + \frac{\sum_{u_a \in \mathcal{S}_n(u_x)} sim(u_x, u_a)(r_{ak} - \bar{r}_a)}{\sum_{u_a \in \mathcal{S}_n(u_x)} sim(u_x, u_a)} \tag{3.4}$$

where $sim(u_x, u_a)$ is a similarity measure between users u_x and u_a such as Cosine similarity or Pearson's correlation coefficient. An item list, $\mathcal{S}_i(u_x)$, can be produced for the active user by sorting the items according the predicted rating scores in descending order and then selecting top-L items[1]. This technique is also known as *memory-based* CF since it requires all ratings, items, and users be stored in memory.

The user centric CF methods can be adopted for Web page recommendation. Since explicit ratings of users to Web pages are usually not available, the CF methods for Web page recommendation work with implicit rating data. The rating matrix of a Web page recommender system based on CF techniques can be formed in two different ways. The first one is a user-page matrix, where the rows and columns correspond to users and Web pages, respectively. The value of each page in the user-page matrix can be the total amount of time that a particular user spends on the page in all of her sessions. These values should be normalized across the visiting times of the pages visited by a user. This normalization captures the relative importance of a page to a user. The normalization could also be done across the visiting times of a single page to capture the relative weight of that page for a specific user, with respect to the weights of the same page for all other users. The recommendations for an active user u_a are generated based on the preferences of most similar users to u_a where the similarity between users can be calculated using Eq. 3.2 or Eq. 3.3.

The second method involves a session-page matrix as a rating matrix where the rows and columns correspond to user sessions and Web pages, respectively. A Web page recommender system based on user centric CF techniques usually employs session-page matrix, which is constructed as explained in Section 2.5. In this case, it is assumed that users may be interested in different topics in their different sessions. For each user session, the recommendation system finds the most similar user sessions. Similarities between user sessions are calculated using one of the similarity measures given in Eq. 3.2 or Eq. 3.3 where a user session is a vector over the space of pages in a Web site. Given a user's current session, the system generates recommendations specific to that session. The active user session can be incrementally updated as the user visits additional pages on the Web site. Alternatively, the last k pages of the active user session as a sliding window can be used to generate recommendations. This method may be more appropriate for Web page recommendation since most users navigate several paths leading to independent pieces of information within a session [Mobasher et al., 2001b].

---

[1]Note that L denotes the number of items whereas K denotes the number of users.

User centric CF methods have been used effectively for Web page recommendation. However, sparsity of session-page matrix is an important problem for recommender systems based on CF techniques. Most users do not visit most Web pages. There may be a small set of popular Web pages which are visited by most of the users. Although CF based recommendation models may produce very satisfying results in this case, it becomes prone to "popularity bias", recommending items that are correct recommendations but quite obvious. A simple search query can also find popular pages easily. Thus, the probability of finding a set of novel, but relevant, pages as a recommendation set is usually low with a sparse data set.

In addition to the limitations mentioned above, another difficult, though common problem of CF systems is the cold-start problem, where recommendations are required for Web pages that are added new to the Web site and no one in the data set has yet visited. The lack of page weights as well as the sparseness and the large volume of data pose limitations to standard CF. As a result, it becomes hard to scale CF techniques to a large number of Web pages while maintaining reasonable prediction performance and accuracy. Most importantly, calculating the neighbors of a user is a time and memory consuming task since it requires all the calculations to make in real-time while keeping the data in memory. Thus, in a pure memory-based CF algorithm, the time and memory requirements scale linearly with the number of users and pages. For a Web site with many Web pages and users who wish to receive recommendations in a small fraction of a second, it would be immensely resource intensive to scan the ratings of many users to return a recommendation in this short period of time. A number of optimization strategies have been proposed and employed to remedy these shortcomings of CF techniques. Pattern discovery techniques have been proposed to address some of the limitations of collaborative methods. Clustering algorithms have been widely used to quickly find a user's neighbors [Mobasher et al., 2001b; Ungar and Foster, 1998]. The users or sessions represented with pages as features are clustered by using any clustering algorithm. Clustering of users or sessions enables to reduce the similarity search space and the time for producing the recommendation set. The details of this method will be discussed in Section 3.3.

Item Centric Collaborative Filtering: Although CF approaches are mainly used to find similar users (or session), they may also be used to find similar items (note that the items correspond to Web page in a Web page recommender system). To overcome the shortcomings of memory-based methods, such as scalability, item-based CF methods were developed [Sarwar et al., 2001]. One of the most famous of the current recommendation systems nowadays is the Amazon.com Recommendation [Linden et al., 2003]. This recommendation system incorporates a matrix of the item similarity. The formulation of the matrix is performed off-line. The intuition behind this approach is that a user may be interested in items similar to the items that she liked earlier. This approach looks at the items that an active user has liked and finds the most similar items to those as a recommendation set. Thus, an item-item matrix is computed from the user-item matrix to represent the similarities between items. By using the transpose of the $(n \times m)$ user-item matrix, the items are converted into vectors in the n-dimensional user space. The pair-wise similarities between items can be calculated using the Cosine similarity between item vectors or Pearson correlation coefficient between two items. As in finding top-K similar users, for each item i_c, a set of top-K items similar to item i_c, denoted as $S_n(i_c)$, can be generated, and their corresponding similarities are recorded.

In the prediction step, for each user u_x who has rated a set of items $S(u_x)$, a candidate set C of items are generated by taking the union of all the set of items $S_n(i_c)$, for each item, $i_c \in S(u_x)$, and then removing the items that are already in $S(u_x)$. The recommendation score of each item $i_m \in C$ for user u_x is calculated as follows [Deshpande and Karypis, 2004; Linden et al., 2003; Sarwar et al., 2001]:

$$\widehat{r}_{xm} = \frac{\sum_{i_j \in S_n(i_m)} sim(i_m, i_j) * r_{aj}}{\sum_{i_b \in S_n(i_m)} sim(i_m, i_b)} \tag{3.5}$$

where $sim(i_m, i_b)$ is the item similarity calculated by the Cosine measure or Pearson correlation coefficient.

One of the potential drawbacks of this approach is the use of raw similarities between items since the neighbors of items are of different density. As a result, the raw similarity between each item i_m and the items in the set of $S_n(i_m)$ may be significantly different [Deshpande and Karypis, 2004]. For this reason, the similarities of an item i_m are normalized such that they add up to one.

Although the drawback due to the sparseness of the data can be overcome by applying an item-based CF recommender system, the cold-start problem still remains unsolved. It is very difficult to generate recommendations for a user without existent ratings or to recommend an item which has not been rated yet. In case of a Web page recommendation, where the session-page matrix is applied as a rating matrix, the prediction for a user who visits the Web site for the first time would not cause a problem. However, a new Web page added to the Web site is not recommended until a user visits it. To solve this problem, content based filtering approaches are recommended.

Content-based Collaborative Filtering: A different approach to CF is content-based filtering method, which provides recommendations by matching user profiles with descriptions of the items. It is reasonable to expect that items with similar features will be almost equally interesting to users. Content based CF systems can be considered as a hybrid system in the sense that it combines the features associated with items and the ratings that a user has given them. In content based recommendation methods, the utility $g(u_k, i_c)$ of an item i_c for user u_k is estimated based on the utilities $g(u_k, i_m)$ of items that are "similar" to item i_c. The utility $g(u_k, i_m)$ of an item i_m for a user u_k is measured based on the rating given by u_k to that item. The similarity between items is calculated using the content description of items.

In general, content-based CF recommendation systems recommend an item to a user based on a description of the item and a profile of the user's interests. While a user profile may be entered by the user, it is commonly learned from feedback the user provides on items, i.e., ratings). A variety of learning algorithms have been adapted to learning user profiles, and the choice of learning algorithm depends on the representation of content [Pazzani and Billsus, 2007].

In content based Web page recommendation models, the session-page matrix is employed as rating matrix. In order to recommend a set of Web pages to user u_k, the content-based recommender system tries to understand the commonalities among the pages user u_k visited in her current session (keywords, titles, etc.). Then, only the pages that have a high degree of content similarity to the pages the user has visited in the same session would be recommended. The content-based approach to Web page recommendation has its roots in information retrieval [Baeza-Yates and Ribeiro-Neto, 1999], since the content of Web pages are represented as the terms that appear on pages. The content of a Web page can be extracted as explained in Section 2.4, and it can be represented by a set of keywords using VSM. However, the performance of the system relies on preprocessing steps to select a manageable set of "important" features from Web page contents. For example, the content of Web pages can be represented by m keywords with the highest TF-IDF weight [Balabanović and Shoham, 1997]. The importance can also be determined by the expected information gain [Quinlan, 1986], $E(t_j, \mathcal{P})$ of a keyword t_j with respect to the usefulness of it in the classification of a set of documents $\mathcal{P}$ where the class labels of documents are available [Pazzani and Billsus, 1997]:

$$E(t_j, \mathcal{P}) = I(\mathcal{P}) - [p(t_j = present)I(\mathcal{P}_{t_j=present}) + p(t_j = absent)I(\mathcal{P}_{t_j=absent})] \quad (3.6)$$

where

$$I(\mathcal{P}) = \sum_c p(\mathcal{P}_c) \log_2(p(\mathcal{P}_c)) \quad (3.7)$$

and $p(t_j = present)$ is the probability that t_j is present in a document, and $\mathcal{P}_{t_j=present}$ is the set of documents that contain at least one occurrence of t_j and $\mathcal{P}_c$ is the documents that belong to class c. The top-m keyword that have the highest expected information gain can be used to represent documents.

Once a representation has been found for Web pages in terms of keywords, a page-keyword matrix can be constructed (Fig. 2.6(a)). Thus, a server session is associated with the keywords of the Web pages that are visited in the session. As in a general content-based recommender system, a profile is learned from the keywords of the pages to model the interest of a user in a session. When an active visitor starts a new session in the Web site, the navigation pattern after a few clicks is identified, and the recommendation score is computed by measuring the similarity of the keywords of the pages the user visited with those not being visited, to determine which attributes might be potentially interesting to the same user.

Most of the CF approaches are developed for recommending items such as books, movies or CDs, rather than Web pages on a Web site. As explained in Section 2, the Web access logs are usually collected anonymously. Thus, the entire behavior of a user in a Web site is not directly available. The user behavior can be modeled in terms of user sessions and the session-page matrix can be used as a rating matrix in CF systems. Furthermore, the values of this matrix, namely the rating values, can be obtained indirectly as a function of time that a user spends on a Web page. The memory-based CF approaches are hard to scale, and the online prediction time complexity of these approaches is high. CF based techniques do not consider the sequence of visiting pages in modeling the behavior of a user in a session. Given a portion of the user session, CF approaches can predict a set of pages that a user may visit in the remaining part of her session. This makes them less efficient when the aim is to predict the Web page that a user will visit next.

3.2   ASSOCIATION RULES

Association rules capture the relationships among items based on their patterns of co-occurrence across transactions. The problem of discovering association rules was introduced by Agrawal et al. [1993]. Given a set $\mathcal{D}$ of transactions, where each transaction is a set of items, an association rule is an expression of the form $X \Rightarrow Y$, where X (defined as the left-hand-side (LHS) of the association rule) and Y (defined as the right-hand-side (RHS) of the association rule) are sets of items such that no item appears more than once in $X \cup Y$. The intuitive meaning of such a rule is that transactions in the database that contain the items in X tend to also contain the items in Y. For example, $\{milk, bread\} \Rightarrow eggs$, is an association rule meaning that customers who buy milk and bread are also likely to purchase eggs. Two common numeric measures assigned to each association rule are *support* and *confidence* to measure the significance of an association rule. Support quantifies how often the items in X and Y occur together in the same transaction as a fraction of the total number of transactions:

$$support = \frac{|X \cup Y|}{|\mathcal{D}|} \tag{3.8}$$

where $|\mathcal{D}|$ denotes the total number of transactions. If the support of an itemset X with k items satisfies a prespecified minimum support threshold, then X is a frequent $k-$itemset. Confidence quantifies how often X and Y occur together as a fraction of the number of transactions in which X occurs:

$$confidence = \frac{|X \cup Y|}{|X|} \tag{3.9}$$

The problem of finding association rules is that of the mining of all rules existing in a transaction database $\mathcal{D}$ with respect to minimal thresholds on support and confidence measures. The Apriori algorithm is one of the first methods to find association rules [Agrawal et al., 1993]. It consists of two steps: (1) find all frequent itemsets that are defined as sets of items with a support value exceeding a predefined threshold value and (2) generate high confidence rules. In the first step, Apriori algorithm employs an iterative approach where frequent $k-$itemsets are obtained from frequent $(k - 1)-$itemsets. First, the transaction data set is scanned to find the set of frequent 1-itemsets. Next, this set is used to find the set of frequent 2-itemsets, and so on, until no more frequent itemsets are found. This step is based on the property that all nonempty subsets of a frequent itemset must also be frequent. This property also describes as being anti-monotonic, in that, if an itemset does not satisfy the minimum support requirement, all of its supersets will also not satisfy this requirement. Thus, if an itemset is infrequent, all of its supersets must be infrequent, and vice versa. The association rule algorithms based on this Apriori property have high computational complexity since they need to repeatedly scan the database for finding each frequent $k-$itemset. To further enhance the scalability of association rule mining, a method called FP-tree was proposed [Han et al., 2000] to find frequent itemsets. During recent years, many algorithms for specialized tasks, such as quantitative association rules, have been developed [Hipp et al., 2000].

In the context of Web usage mining, association rules refer to sets of pages that are accessed together with a support value exceeding some specified threshold. These pages may not be directly connected to one another via hyperlinks. For example, using association rule discovery techniques, one can find correlations such as the following:

- 40% of users visit the Web page with URL /home/page1, and the Web Page with URL /home/page2 in the same user session.

- 30% of users who accessed the Web page with URL /home/products, also accessed /home/products/computers.

There are successful approaches that use generated association rules for Web page prediction [Forsati and Meybodi, 2010; Huang et al., 2002; Mobasher et al., 2001c; Yan and Li, 2006]. Once the user sessions are extracted from server logs, association rules can be generated from this set of user sessions S. In this dataset, the page weights $w_{p_j^m}$ of a session vector s_m will be binary values: 0 if the page p_j is not visited during the session, 1, otherwise. When using page weight as a function of time spent at a page, a weighted association rule algorithm [Tao et al., 2003] can be used. Thus, in this step, an (weighted) association rule algorithm can be employed to extract association rules from the set of sessions. To illustrate the process, consider the sample dataset in Table 2.4. The itemsets generated from this set of user sessions using Apriori algorithm with a minimum support threshold of 2 are given in Table 3.1 (the support of each set is given in parentheses). Recall that p_i corresponds to a page, so each entry in Table 3.1 indicates frequently accessed pages (for size 1) and pages that are frequently accessed together (when size is higher).

Table 3.1: Frequent itemsets of the sample dataset generated by the Apriori algorithm

Size 1	Size 2	Size 3
$\{p_1\}$ (3)	$\{p_1, p_3\}$ (2)	$\{p_1, p_3, p_4\}$ (2)
$\{p_3\}$ (2)	$\{p_1, p_4\}$ (3)	
$\{p_4\}$ (3)	$\{p_3, p_4\}$ (2)	

When dealing with Web usage data, the frequency of top level navigation pages may be higher than the frequency of low level pages in the site hierarchy that contain more specific information. For this reason, an algorithm which allows users to set multiple support values for different items may be preferable, for it captures patterns and generate recommendations that contain these less frequent pages [Liu et al., 1999].

The recommendation engine uses the resulting frequent items (pages) to make a recommendation according to the user's actions. A fixed-size sliding window over the current active session is used to capture the current user's behavior. For example, if the current session (with a window size of 3) is $\langle p_1, p_2, p_3 \rangle$, and the user references the page p_4, then the new active session becomes $\langle p_2, p_3, p_4 \rangle$. The recommendation engine matches the current user session window with frequent pages to find candidate pages for giving recommendations. Given an active session window w, all frequent itemsets of size $w + 1$, which contain the active user session window are considered. The recommendation score of each candidate page is calculated using the confidence value of the corresponding association rule whose right-hand side is the singleton containing the page to be recommended. If the rule satisfies a user specified confidence threshold, then the candidate page is added to the recommendation set. To improve the recommendation efficiency, the extracted itemsets can be stored in a directed, acyclic graph [Mobasher et al., 2001a] called a *Frequent Itemset Graph*. The graph is an extension of the lexicographic tree used in the tree projection algorithm [Agarwal et al., 2001]. The lexicographic tree is a structural representation of the frequent itemsets with respect to the lexicographic ordering. In this tree, each node corresponds to a frequent itemset where the root node corresponds to the empty itemset. The levels in a lexicographic tree correspond to the sizes of the different itemsets. Thus, a node in the graph at level d contains an itemset, X, of size d sorted in lexicographic order and is linked to a node at depth $d + 1$, containing an itemset $X \cup \{p\}$ where p is a Web page. Fig. 3.4 shows the graph constructed for the frequent itemsets of the example dataset.

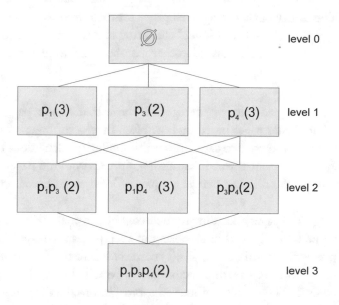

Figure 3.4: The Frequent Itemsets Graph for the example dataset

The active user session, s_a with a window size of w, is sorted in lexicographic order to be able to match different ordering with frequent itemsets. If a match is found at level w of the graph, then the children nodes of the matching node containing s_a are used to generate recommendations.

Each child node of a matching node consists of an itemset $s_a \cup \{p\}$. The page p is added to the recommendation set if the confidence value of the association rule $s_a \Rightarrow p$ exceeds a user defined threshold. The confidence of this rule is also used as the recommendation score for page p. Note that, since sets are not ordered, when using a recommender model based on frequent itemsets, the sequence of page requests in an active user session is not considered. Before generating recommendations, each active user session is sorted in lexicographic order. The recommendation set for an active user is generated from the itemsets that contain the active user session. Thus, this kind of recommender models may result in low accuracy in predicting the next request of a user given her previous request in a session.

3.3   CLUSTERING

Clustering is a technique to group together a set of items with similar characteristics. In the Web usage domain, there are three kinds of interesting clusters to be discovered: (1) session clusters, (2) user clusters, and (3) page clusters. Session clustering implementation allows clustering of user sessions in which users have similar access patterns. In most of the Web page prediction applications, it is difficult to form user clusters due to the lack of data about users. For this reason, sessions or Web pages are clustered. Clustering of users tends to establish groups of users exhibiting similar browsing patterns. The utility of clustering Web pages for the purpose of Web page prediction lies in so called cluster hypothesis: given a "suitable" clustering of a collection, if the user is interested in a Web page p_i, she is likely to be interested in other members of the cluster to which p_i belongs.

3.3.1   PAGE CLUSTERS

Page clustering can be grouped into two categories: those that cluster pages according to their contents, and those that cluster pages based on how often they occur together across user sessions. The main difference between these two categories is the similarity calculations between Web pages. Similarity measure plays an essential role in clustering. To perform Web page clustering, similarity measures often determine the distance between a pair of Web pages based on the feature vectors describing them.

When clustering Web pages according to their content, an analysis of the content of Web site is needed. The data type typically used in clustering of Web pages is the matrix expression of data. The ith row in the page-term matrix in Fig. 2.6(a) corresponds to the feature vector of a Web page p_i as in Eq. 2.1. The terms in this feature vector can be extracted from the content of Web pages as explained in Chapter 2. There are a number of approaches in the literature for data clustering. These approaches can be categorized as partitioning methods, hierarchical methods, density-based methods, grid-based methods, model-based methods, high-dimensional clustering and constraint-based clustering [Han and Kamber, 2006]. Clustering algorithms based on partitioning methods assign n data objects into k disjoint clusters where $k \ll n$. The well-known *k-means* clustering is one of the most popular statistical clustering techniques for analyzing Web page content. It is a simple algorithm, the pseudocode for which can be found in Algorithm 2 [Han and Kamber, 2006]. Once the feature vectors of Web pages are obtained, the Web pages can be clustered by using a traditional clustering method, such as k-means.

Content data can be enriched with "additional data", such as anchor texts and extended anchor texts (the window consisting of text surrounding the anchor text). These additional data have been shown more useful than, or, in some cases, at least as useful as Web page content in describing the content of Web pages and clustering of them [Glover et al., 2002]. It is argued that the extended anchor texts of a page better summarize the content of it since people providing them are interested in the page. This argument was supported by the experimental results which indicate that extended anchor texts have greater descriptive power than both page content and anchor texts in describing clusters. Before clustering, each Web page was converted into a set of features that occurred in its extended anchor text. The feature vector from each extended anchor text of a page are equally weighted in aggregating a feature vector for the page. For example, suppose that there are two links pointing to a Web page p_i. The first extended anchor text is converted into a feature vector $E_{i1} = \langle computer, program, language \rangle$, where the second one is converted into the feature vector $E_{i2} = \langle program, language, java \rangle$. The weights of these terms are binary. The Web page p_i can then be represented by a feature vector $p_i = \langle (1, computer), (2, program), (2, language), (1, java) \rangle$ where the weight of each term is calculated by adding the weights of each occurrence of that term in each feature vector of the page's extended anchor text.

Algorithm 2 The k-means algorithm

Input : k: the number of clusters, $\mathcal{D}$: a data set containing n objects
Output : A set of k clusters

1: arbitrarily choose k objects from $\mathcal{D}$ as the initial cluster centers;
2: **repeat**
3:    (re)assign each object to the cluster to which the object is the most similar, based on the mean value of the objects in the cluster;
4:    update the cluster means, i.e., calculate the mean value of the objects for each cluster;
5: **until** no change

The feature vector from each extended anchor text of a page can also be weighted by the in-link strength in aggregating a feature vector for the page [Zhu et al., 2004]. User traversals on the in-links of a Web page are used to represent the in-link strength of that page. Figure 3.5 shows the link structure of a Web site. Some pages can have multiple in-links, such as p_{11}, which has in-links from pages p_5, p_6 and p_7. Fig. 3.6 shows the in-link strength matrix of this Web site, in which each entry represents the in-link strength of the link, from the page indexed by the row, to the page indexed by the column. In this example, when constructing the feature vector of page p_{11}, the terms coming from extended anchor text on pages p_5, p_6 and p_7 are weighted by 0.413, 0.305 and 0.282, respectively. If a term appears in more than one extended anchor text, then this term appears only once in the resulting feature vector of the page where its total weight is summed up.

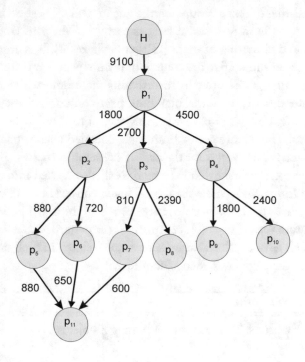

Figure 3.5: The links in a Web site and numbers of traversals on these links [Zhu et al., 2004]

	p_1	p_2	p_3	p_4	p_5	p_6	p_7	p_8	p_9	p_{10}	p_{11}
p_1		1	1	1							
p_2					1	1					
p_3							1	1			
p_4									1	1	
p_5											0.413
p_6											0.305
p_7											0.282
p_8											
p_9											
p_{10}											
p_{11}											

Figure 3.6: The in-link strength matrix of the link hierarchy shown in Figure 3.5 [Zhu et al., 2004].

One of the commonly used similarity functions in information retrieval (e.g., Cosine similarity or Euclidean distance) can be employed for similarity calculations. Once the similarities are calculated between Web pages, they can be clustered using an appropriate clustering method.

The similarity between Web pages can also be calculated based on their co-occurrence across user sessions. For M sessions and N pages, a session s_i can be represented by the ith row of the session-page matrix $\mathbf{X}$. Each entry x_{ik} indicates the weight of page p_k in session s_i, where a zero means that the page p_k is not present in that session. Thus, the session-page matrix $\mathbf{X}$ can be decomposed into its row vectors:

$$\mathbf{X} = [s_1, \ldots, s_M]^T, \quad s_m = [x_{m1}, \ldots, x_{mN}], \quad m = 1, \ldots, M \tag{3.10}$$

where each row represent a session in terms of requested Web pages in this session. Alternatively, the matrix can also be represented by its column vectors:

$$\mathbf{X} = [p_1, \ldots, p_N], \quad p_k = [x_{1k}, \ldots, x_{Mk}], \quad k = 1, \ldots, K \tag{3.11}$$

where each column vector p_k corresponds to a specific Web page's usage in all user sessions.

Similarity between two Web pages can be measured in different ways. One way is to calculate Cosine similarity or Euclidean distance between each pair of column vectors in session-page matrix $\mathbf{X}$. Another method is counting the number of co-occurrences, that is, the number of times when two Web pages are requested, in the same session. Let A and B be the sets of user sessions in which page p_i and p_j are requested, respectively, relative co-occurrence is defined as:

$$RC(p_i, p_j) = \frac{|A \cap B|}{|A \cup B|} \tag{3.12}$$

That is, relative co-occurrence is equal to the division between the number of sessions in which pages co-occur, and the number of sessions in which appears any one of two pages. For clustering, a similarity graph can be formed where the nodes represent Web pages and the weighted, undirected edges represent strength of similarity, based on the number of page co-occurrences. One of the well known graph clustering algorithms, such as Girvan-Newman algorithm [Girvan and Newman, 2002] can be applied for graph clustering. The pseudo code of this algorithm is given in Algorithm 3.

In this algorithm, the betweenness of an edge is calculated by the number of shortest paths connecting any pair of vertices that pass through the edge. For a graph $G = (V, E)$ where V is the set of vertices and E is the set of edges, the betweenness $C_B(e)$ for edge e is:

$$C_B(e) = \sum_{s \neq v \neq t \in V} \frac{\sigma_{st}(e)}{\sigma_{st}} \tag{3.13}$$

where σ_{st} is the number of shortest paths from s to t, and $\sigma_{st}(e)$ is the number of shortest paths from s to t that pass through an edge e. The reason of removing edges with high betweenness values is that edges that lie on many shortest paths between nodes in the graph have high betweenness.

These edges lie in sparse parts of the graph connecting two clusters, so high betweenness indicates the boundary between clusters.

Fig. 3.7 shows an example of a hierarchical tree obtained by clustering a graph with 12 vertices. The circles at the bottom of the figure represent the vertices in the graph and the tree shows the order in which they join together to form clusters. Selection of k clusters from such a hierarchical clustering corresponds to cutting the dendogram with a horizontal line at an appropriate height, which yields k branches. For example, cutting the dendogram at the level of dashed line in Fig. 3.7 results in five clusters.

Algorithm 3 The Girvan-Newman algorithm

Input : $\mathcal{G}$: an undirected weighted graph
Output : A set of k clusters

1: calculate the betweenness of all existing edges in the graph;
2: **repeat**
3:      remove the edges with the highest betweenness;
4:      recalculate the betweenness of all edges affected by the removal;
5: **until** no edges remain

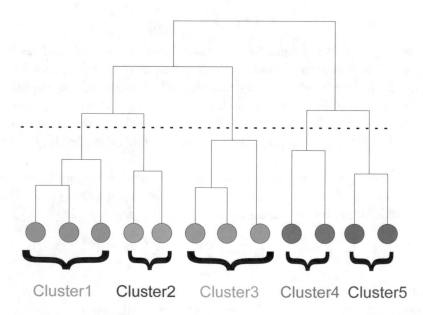

Figure 3.7: An example of a small hierarchical clustering tree.

To utilize the clusters in the recommendation step, the profile of each cluster should be extracted. Mean of each cluster stands for the profile of the corresponding cluster, which is given by a vector obtained by calculating the mean values of all data points assigned to that particular cluster.

However, for accurately recommending Web pages to users, clusters of Web pages based on their content are not sufficient. For this reason, the clusters of Web pages are then used for preprocessing Web user sessions obtained from log data to generate more accurate recommendations. In the on-line step of the recommendation model, recommendations are generated by two different methods: (1) by matching the active user sessions against user profiles obtained by applying different data mining tasks such as association rules or sequential patterns and (2) by matching the current active session against all content profiles represented as cluster centers. Two recommendation sets can be combined by just taking the union of them or if it is possible to calculate a recommendation value for each page in both of the recommendation sets. A set of pages with the maximum recommendation value across the two recommendation sets can be presented as a recommendation [Mobasher et al., 2000]. This is called the hybrid recommendation method [Burke, 2002]. The combination in such a system happens only in the on-line phase.

Usage data and content data can also be combined in an off-line phase of the recommendation process. After clustering Web pages based on their contents, the resulting clusters are used to examine the discovered Web sessions in order to identify *missions* [Zaïane et al., 2004]. A mission is defined as a sub-session with a consistent goal. These missions are in turn clustered to generate navigational patterns. In clustering phase, a soft clustering method is applied, which allows the ability to determine the size of clusters and assigns Web pages to more than one cluster. Suppose the text clustering algorithm groups Web pages p_1, p_2, p_3 and p_5, Web pages p_1, p_2, p_3 and p_6, and Web pages p_1, p_3 and p_4 into three different content clusters. Then for a visit session: p_1, p_2, p_3, p_4, p_5, the proposed system identifies three missions as follows: mission 1: (p_1, p_2, p_3, p_5); mission 2: (p_1, p_2, p_3, p_6); and mission 3: (p_1, p_3, p_4). The Web sessions are divided into missions and these missions are in turn clustered to generate navigational patterns. Each page in a cluster is represented in a keyword vector to compute the topic vector of each cluster, in which the value of a keyword is the average of the corresponding values of all pages in the cluster. When a visitor starts a new session in the Web site, the contextual topic of interest of the visitor is identified after a few clicks using the anchor clicked by the current user and its neighborhood on either side. The captured topics are also represented by a keyword vector which is matched on-the-fly with already captured navigational patterns. If they were matched, the most relevant pages in the matched cluster are recommended to the visitor.

3.3.2   SESSION CLUSTERS

Clustering techniques can also be used for grouping similar user sessions. The aim of this clustering for Web page recommendation is to find user groups with similar behavior in a Web site. In the recommendation step, the session of an active user is assigned to the cluster that is found to be most similar to the active user session. Then the recommendation set is generated based on the user sessions in the most similar cluster. Thus, besides the clustering technique in the off-line step, it is also important to select the most similar cluster and generate a recommendation set in the on-line step. Moreover, the speed of the recommendation engine is of great importance in on-line recommendation systems. Clustering of user sessions will accelerate the process of the recommendation set generation since this set is generated using a smaller number of sessions that reside in the most similar cluster. Many recommendation models ignore detailed sequence and time information during clustering in order to save space and time. We first consider recommendation models in which user sessions are represented as feature vectors of Web pages.

The user session data are modeled as matrix (Fig. 2.6(b)) where the weights associated with Web pages can be determined based on time spent on that page. Various clustering algorithms have been used, including partitioning algorithms such as K-means for user session clustering [Mobasher et al., 2001b]. The clustering algorithm partitions user sessions in a multidimensional space as vectors of pages into groups of sessions that are close to each other based on a measure of distance or similarity. Such a clustering yields a set of clusters $C = \{c_1, \ldots, c_r\}$, where each c_t is subset of the set if user sessions. Each cluster represents the behavior of a particular subgroup.

The usage pattern for each cluster is represented by the center of that cluster. The center of a cluster c_t can be computed easily by calculating the mean vectors of the sessions assigned to the cluster:

$$\vec{\mu_t} = \langle w_{p_1}, w_{p_2}, \ldots, w_{p_N} \rangle$$

where w_{p_j} is given by

$$w_{p_j} = \frac{1}{|c_t|} \cdot \sum_{s_i \in c_t} w_{p_{ij}}$$

where $|c_t|$ is the number of user sessions in cluster c_t.

In the recommendation step, a similarity value is calculated between each cluster center $\vec{\mu_t}$ and the active user session $\vec{s_a}$ using the cosine similarity metric. The cluster with the highest similarity value, $sim(\vec{s_a}, \vec{\mu_t})$, is selected as the best matching cluster. To recommend pages, the recommendation algorithm uses the center vector of the best matching cluster. A recommendation score is calculated by multiplying each weight in the cluster center vector by the similarity value of that cluster. The recommendation score of a page $p_i \in \mathcal{P}$ is calculated as follows:

$$rec(\vec{s_a}, p_i) = \sqrt{w(p_i) \times sim(\vec{s_a}, \vec{\mu_t})}$$

The first k pages with the highest recommendation scores are added to the individual recommendation set of this model.

Next, we consider recommendation models based on clustering user sessions represented as Web page sequences. Clustering user sessions is one of the widely used techniques in Web usage mining to group similar sessions, and different clustering algorithms are designed for this purpose. It is important to select a clustering method such that the resulting clusters are appropriate to use in the recommendation step. Another issue is to effectively represent each cluster to utilize them in the on-line step for assigning the active user session to the most similar cluster and then generating a recommendation set using that cluster. The solution of these problems is straightforward when representing user sessions as vectors of pages and employing clustering methods that require a metric space. However, in this case, the sequence information is lost. Thus, although this type of recommender systems are easy to implement and maintain, they are less effective when predicting the next request of users, compared to the models that are based on the information of the sequence features of user sessions.

Clustering is usually used with other data mining techniques in Web page prediction. For example, in recent years, there are several approaches to combine these clustering methods with association rules and Markov models [Khalil et al., 2008]. For accurately predicting the next page of an active user session, the clustering methods that work on sequence data are more appropriate. The recommendation models based on sequence clustering methods will be explained in the next section after describing the sequence properties and sequence data in Web usage mining.

3.4   SEQUENTIAL PATTERNS

The sequential pattern mining problem was first introduced in [Agrawal and Srikant, 1995]. Given a set of sequences, where each sequence consists of a list of elements and each element consists of a set of items, and given a user specified *min_support* threshold, sequential pattern mining finds all of the frequent subsequences, i.e., the subsequences whose occurrence frequency in the set of sequences is no less than *min_support*.

In Web server logs, a visit of a user is recorded over a period of time. A time stamp can be attached either to the user session or to the individual page requests of user sessions. By analyzing this information with sequential pattern discovery methods, the Web mining system can determine temporal relationships among data items such as the following:

- 30% of users who visited /home/products/dvd/movies, had visited /home/ products/games within the past week.

- 40% of users request the page with URL /home/products/monitors after visiting the page /home/products/computers.

Sequential patterns in Web usage data capture the Web page trails that are often visited by users, in the order that they were visited. Sequential patterns are those sequences of items that frequently occur in a sufficiently large proportion of sessions. Although some of the models explained in this subsection use additional data mining techniques such as clustering, they are categorized under the models based on sequential patterns. The reason for this is that they represent user sessions as sequences.

Since its introduction, sequential pattern mining is an important data mining problem with broad applications, including the analysis of customer purchase behavior, Web access patterns, scientific experiments, disease treatments, natural disasters, DNA sequences, and so on. Let Σ be a finite alphabet of characters or symbols. The number of distinct characters in the alphabet is denoted as $|\Sigma|$. A sequence of length l is called a $l-$sequence, which is a string or word w of length l drawn from the alphabet Σ.

Markov-based models have been extensively used to study the stochastic processes, and are naturally well-suited for modeling sequential processes, such as browsing a Web site. Let s be the $l-$sequence drawn from the alphabet $\Sigma = \{A, C, G, T\}$. For example, a $5-$sequence s might be $ACTTG$. The probability of generating the sequence s is [Baldi et al., 2003]:

$$P(s) = P(s_1) \prod_{t=2}^{l} P(s_t | s_{t-1}, \ldots, s_1) \tag{3.14}$$

where s_t is the state at position t in the sequence, $1 \leq t \leq l$. Under a first-order Markov assumption, it is assumed that the probability of each state s_t, given the preceding states $s_{t-1}, \ldots, s_1$, only depends on state s_{t-1}:

$$P(s) = P(s_1) \prod_{t=2}^{l} P(s_t | s_{t-1}) \tag{3.15}$$

A sequence is produced under the first-order Markov assumption by first selecting an initial state s_1 from a distribution $P(s_1)$, then given s_1 selecting the state s_2 from the distribution $P(s_2|s_1)$, and so on. The transition matrix T is defined as an $M \times M$ matrix with M states where $T_{ij} = P(s_t = j | s_{t_1} = i)$ the probability of transitioning from state i to state j and $\sum_{j=1}^{M} T_{ij} = 1$.

Returning to the issue of modeling how a user navigates a Web site, the alphabet Σ corresponds to the set of Web pages $\mathcal{P} = \{p_1, p_2, \ldots, p_N\}$ in the Web site. Each Web page in $\mathcal{P}$ corresponds to a state in the Markov model. Markov models are widely used predicting Web users' sequential browsing behaviors since the early approaches where a first order Markov model was employed in order to predict the users' next requests [Bestavros, 1995]. A prediction model is obtained from the access patterns of previous users. To improve the performance of the recommendation model, the first order Markov model is enhanced with the use of a hybrid prediction model [Zukerman et al., 1999].

A Hypertext Probabilistic Automaton (HPA) was proposed to model the users' interaction with a Web site [Borges and Levene, 1999]. From the set of user sessions in the Web log, we can identify the number of times a Web page was requested, the number of times it was the first page in the sessions and the number of times it was the last page. The number of times a sequence of $p_i \rightarrow p_j$ appears in the sessions gives the number of times the users followed a link from p_i towards p_j. A parameter α is introduced into the model in order to give an initial probability to every Web page greater than zero when $\alpha > 0$.

Example 1 In the set of sample user session in Table 3.2, there are 24 page requests in 6 user sessions, wherein page p_1 is requested 4 times with 2 times as the first request of a session. Fig. 3.8 shows the corresponding hypertext grammar of the sessions in Table 3.2. In this figure, each

SID	User Session
1	p_1, p_2, p_3, p_4
2	p_1, p_5, p_3, p_4, p_1
3	p_5, p_2, p_4, p_6
4	p_5, p_2, p_3
5	p_5, p_2, p_3, p_6
6	p_4, p_1, p_5, p_3

Table 3.2: A set of sample user sessions

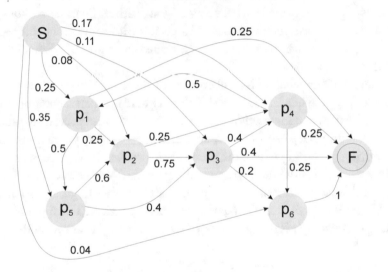

Figure 3.8: The hypertext grammar extracted from the set of session in Table 3.2 for $N = 1$ and $\alpha = 0.5$

non-terminal state corresponds to a Web page on the Web site. There are two additional states, S and F, which correspond the start and finish states of the sessions, respectively. Since $\alpha = 0.5$, the initial probability of page p_1 is $P(p_1) = \frac{0.5 \cdot 4}{24} + \frac{0.5 \cdot 2}{6} = 0.25$.

In an $N-$grammar, it is assumed that only the last visited N pages influence the selection of the next page. From Fig. 3.8, it is apparent that the HPA is equivalent to first order Markov chains, which have been previously used for modeling the user behavior on the Web. Given an HPA, the probability of a string $\omega = p_1 p_2 \ldots p_k$ is denoted by $P(\omega)$ and is calculated as:

$$P(\omega) = P(p_1)P(p_1, p_2) \ldots P(p_{k-1}, p_k) \tag{3.16}$$

where $P(p_i, p_j)$ is the transition probability from page p_i to page p_j. The strings generated by the HPA correspond to the user navigational paths. The navigational paths with high probability can then be used to predict users' next requests. Note that the probability of a string ω is the probability of its path according to the underlying Markov chain.

Markov models are also used with clustering techniques in Web page recommendation [Cadez et al., 2003]. The user sessions represented as sequences of Web pages as in Eq. 2.6 are partitioned into clusters according to the order of Web pages in each session. A model based clustering approach is employed to cluster user sessions. In particular, the user sessions are clustered by learning a mixture of first order Markov models using a standard learning technique, the Expectation-Maximization (EM) algorithm [Dempster et al., 1977]. Each cluster has a different Markov model which consists of a (sparse) matrix of state transition probabilities and the initial state probability vector. The proportion of user sessions assigned to each cluster as well as the parameters of each Markov model are learned using EM algorithm. The user sessions are modeled as follows: (1) a user session is assigned to a particular cluster with some probability and (2) the order of Web pages being requested in that session is generated from a Markov model with parameters specific to that cluster.

The parameters of the Markov Model consists of the probabilities of assigning user sessions to various clusters ($p(c_g)$ where c_g is the gth cluster) and the parameters of each cluster. The parameters of each cluster are composed of a set of states called state space, initial state probabilities, and transition probabilities T_{ij} between two adjacent states x_i and x_j. Each transition entry T_{ij} corresponds of moving to state x_j where the process is in state x_i. In Web page prediction, the state space of the Markov model is the set of pages making up the Web site. A transition probability t_{ij} between state x_i and state x_j corresponds to the probability of visiting page p_j after visiting page p_i ($P(p_j|p_i)$). Let $s_i = (p_1^i, p_2^i, ..., p_m^i)$ be user session of length m. The first order Markov model assumes that the user session s_i is being generated by a mixture of Markov models as follows:

$$P(s_i) = \sum_{g=1}^{G} P(s_i|c_g)p(c_g)$$

$$P(s_i|c_g) = P(p_1^i|c_g) \prod_{j=2}^{m} P(p_j^i|p_{j-1}^i, c_g) \tag{3.17}$$

$$P(c_g|s_i) = \frac{P(s_i|c_g)P(c_g)}{\sum_j P(s_i|c_j)P(c_j)}$$

where G is the number of clusters, and $P(p_1^i|c_g)$ is the initial state probability of the gth cluster for page p_1^i. The parameters of each component are learnt by maximum likelihood estimation. The *maximum likelihood* (ML estimation) approach maximizes:

$$\ell_{ML}(\Theta_1, ..., \Theta_G|D) = \prod_{i=1}^{K} \sum_{g=1}^{G} P(c_g)P(s_i|c_g) \tag{3.18}$$

where Θ_G is the set of parameters of the gth cluster and K is the number of user sessions in the training set used to learn the model parameters.

Since the study in [Cadez et al., 2003] focuses on visualization of navigational patterns rather than on predicting the next request of Web users, the proposed model does not have a recommendation part. An appropriate recommendation engine was developed for this model [Göksedef and Gündüz-Ögüdücü, 2007]. A recommendation set consisting of k pages is generated from this model as follows: The active user session is assigned to one of the clusters (c_a) that has the highest probability calculated using Equation 3.17. The recommendation set for the current user is generated using the transition matrix of c_a. All the transition entries t_{ij} of c_a are sorted in descending order, where the state x_i is equal to the last visited page in the active user session. The top k pages are selected to form a recommendation set.

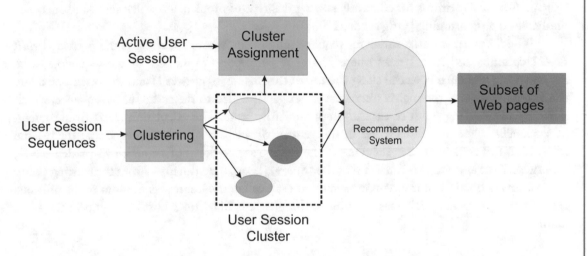

Figure 3.9: The recommendation process of methods based on user session clustering

As mentioned in Section 3.3, clustering is widely used in Web usage mining to group similar user sessions. However, for Web page prediction, it is important to preserve the sequence structure of user sessions during clustering. Fig. 3.9 presents the recommendation process. A clustering algorithm is employed on the session sequences to partition user sessions. The discovered Web user session groups are then represented to create user profiles. When a new active user session is coming, a matching operation is carried out to find the most closest cluster by measuring the similarity between the active user session and the session clusters. Then, the pages in the most matched cluster are selected as the recommendation set according to an algorithm developed in the recommendation engine. Since the structure of sequences makes it difficult to use metric space, clustering methods applicable in metric spaces, such as k-means, are not appropriate for this kind of data. Many sequence clustering algorithms precompute all pairwise sequence similarities. For this reason, several similarity measures are derived by using dynamic programming [Banerjee and Ghosh, 2001; Gündüz-Ögüdücü and Özsu, 2006; Wang and Zaïane, 2002] to calculate pairwise similarities between user sessions. The main idea is to find the overlapping regions (Web pages) between two user sessions. Longest Common Subsequence (LCS) is first found through dynamic programming and then the similarity between on two sessions is calculated based on their relative time spent on the longest common sub-sequences [Banerjee and Ghosh, 2001].

Another approach for similarity calculations between user sessions is based on sequence alignment methods through dynamic programming. For two strings of length m and n, optimal sequence alignment has zero or more gaps inserted into the sequence to maximize the number of positions in the aligned strings that match. For example, consider aligning the sequences "$p_2\ p_8\ p_6\ p_5\ p_3$" and "$p_2\ p_8\ p_4\ p_3$" (Fig. 3.10(a)). By inserting gaps ($-$) in the appropriate place, the number of positions where two sequences match can be maximized. Here the aligned sequences match in three positions (Fig. 3.10(b)). Algorithms for efficiently solving this type of problem are well known and are based on dynamic programming [Driga et al., 2006].

The first step is initialization for sequence alignment, where a scoring matrix is created with $K + 1$ columns and $N + 1$ rows where K and N correspond to the size of the sequences to be aligned. One sequence is placed along the top of the matrix (sequence#1) and the other one along the left-hand-side of the matrix (sequence#2). A gap is added to the end of each sequence, which indicates the starting point of calculation of similarity score. The calculation starts from the end of sequences. There are three scores in this matrix: $Score_{l,r} = s_m$, which means that the residue at position l of sequence #2 is the same as the residue at position r of sequence #1 (match score); otherwise, $Score_{l,r} = s_d$ (mismatch score) or $Score_{l,r} = s_g$ (gap penalty). From the starting point, the last row is filled from right-to-left such that each cell in the last row is the sum of the previous cell and the gap penalty. The last column of the matrix is filled from bottom-to-top in the same manner.

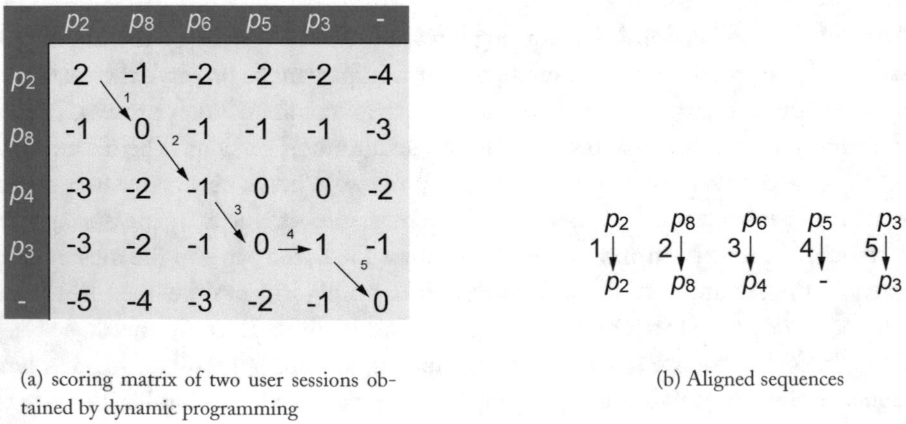

(a) scoring matrix of two user sessions obtained by dynamic programming

(b) Aligned sequences

Figure 3.10: Alignment of two user sessions

Once the sequences are aligned, the next step is to calculate the similarities between Web user sessions. Instead of counting the number of identical Web pages in the aligned session sequences, a scoring function can be created for Web session similarity calculations. In literature, different scoring functions are proposed for this task based on the Web page similarity [Wang and Zaïane, 2002] or based on the time spent on Web pages [Gündüz-Ögüdücü and Özsu, 2006]. After aligning sequences of Web pages, a scoring function based on Web page similarity measure is created. The Web page similarity can be calculated based on the content data on each Web page. It can also be computed by representing each level of a URL by a token; the token string of the full path of a URL is thus the concatenation of all the representative tokens of each level.

Example   2   Consider   two   Web   pages   "/courses/TECH142/index.html"   and "/course/TECH150/description.html". The first one is represented by the token string "001", and the second one is represented by the token string "010". The computation of Web page similarity is based on comparing the token strings of Web pages. Similarity is a value between 0.0 (not similar) to 1.0 (completely similar).

After aligning sequences, the similarity between sessions can also be calculated using the visiting time of pages [Gündüz-Ögüdücü and Özsu, 2006]. This similarity measure has two components, which is defined as *alignment score component* and *local similarity component*. The alignment score component computes how similar the two sessions are in the region of their overlap. If the highest value of the score matrix of two sessions, s_i and s_j, is σ and the number of matching pages is M in the aligned sequence, then the alignment score component is:

$$s_a(s_i, s_j) = \frac{\sigma}{s_m * M} \tag{3.19}$$

The intuition behind this is that score σ is higher if the sessions have more consecutive matching pages. This value is normalized by dividing it by the matching score and the number of matching pages. The local similarity component computes how important the overlap region is. If the length of the aligned sequences is L, the local similarity component is :

$$s_l(S_i, S_j) = \frac{M}{L} \tag{3.20}$$

Then the overall similarity between two sessions is given by

$$sim(s_i, s_j) = s_a(s_i, s_j) * s_l(s_i, s_j) \tag{3.21}$$

For example, the overall similarity between two user sessions whose scoring matrix and alignment are given in Fig. 3.10(a) and Fig. 3.10(b) is $sim(1, 2) = (2/(2 * 3)) * (3/5) = 0.2$.

A session similarity method can be applied to compute the similarity between each pair of sessions, and construct a graph. In this graph, the vertices correspond to user sessions and the edges of the graph are weighted by the similarity values of the corresponding vertices. Proper clustering algorithms, such as graph based clustering algorithms, are then applied to this similarity matrix to find the session clusters [Gündüz-Ögüdücü and Özsu, 2006; Wang and Zaïane, 2002]. A graph based clustering algorithm to compute betweenness values of edges is shown in Algorithm 3.

SID	User Session
1	p_5, p_4 p_3 p_6
2	p_5, p_4, p_3
3	p_5, p_4, p_6
4	p_1, p_5, p_6
5	p_1, p_2, p_8
6	p_2, p_7, p_9
7	p_2, p_8, p_9, p_7
8	p_2, p_8, p_7
8	p_2, p_7, p_9

Table 3.3: A set of user sessions represented as sequences of Web pages

Example 3 Let's consider an example to illustrate the clustering of user sessions represented as Web page sequences. Consider the user sessions given in Table 3.3. After aligning sequences in user sessions the pairwise similarities are calculated and the resulting graph is given in Fig. 3.11. For simplicity, an unweighted graph is constructed. Each edge in the graph assumes an equal weight of 1. Using Equation 3.13, the betweenness values of edges are calculated. Since the edge between s_4 and s_5 (dashed line in the Fig. 3.11) lies on many shortest paths between nodes in the graph, its betweenness value is relatively higher. By removing this edge, the graph is partitioned into two clusters: $\{s_1, s_2, s_3, s_4\}$ and $\{s_5, s_6, s_7, s_8, s_9\}$ another cluster.

Experimental results show that Web page recommendation models that consider the sequence of page requests during the pattern extraction step are more capable of predicting the next requests of Web users [Göksedef and Gündüz-Ögüdücü, 2010].

Although there are several studies for Web session clustering [Banerjee and Ghosh, 2001; Wang and Zaïane, 2002], a few of those studies addressed the problem of Web page prediction. When using clustering methods for grouping user sessions, an important issue is how to represent the resulting clusters efficiently in order to use them in the on-line step of the recommendation model. As explained in Chapter 2, the on-line step of the recommendation model consists of generating a recommendation set for the active user, based on the previous activities of Web users' browsing in the site. In the case of clustering similar user sessions as sequences of Web pages, the on-line step consists of both assigning the active user session to the most similar cluster and then generating

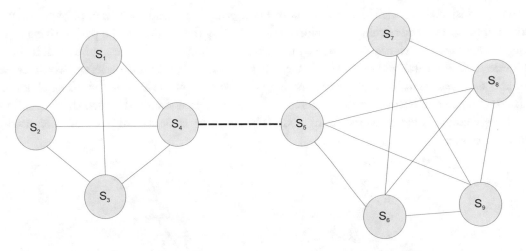

Figure 3.11: The graph constructed from similarity of user sessions in Table 3.3

a recommendation set based on the user sessions in that cluster (Fig. 3.9). For this reason, there are two factors that affect the recommendation accuracy: (1) an efficient clustering method that yields to accurately clustering Web page sequences and (2) an efficient cluster representation, which leads a correct and fast assignment of active user session to the most similar cluster. Proper clustering algorithms for this task are those that work on pairwise similarities of data objects [Demir et al., 2010; Foss et al., 2001; Guha et al., 1999; Karypis et al., 1999]. After dividing user sessions into a number of clusters, Markov model analysis can be carried out on each of the clusters for recommendation set generation. Let $\mathcal{P} = \{p_1, ..., p_N\}$ be a set of pages in a Web site. Let s_a be an active user session including a sequence of l pages visited by the user in a visit. The utility function in Eq. 2.5 to choose a Web page $p' \in \mathcal{P}$ that maximizes the user's utility can be written as:

$$P_{l+1} = \underset{p' \in \mathcal{P}}{\arg\max}\{P(P_{l+1} = p' | p_l, p_{l-1}, \ldots, p_{l-(k-1)})\} \tag{3.22}$$

This probability, $P_{l+1} = P(p' | s_a)$, is estimated by using all sequences of all users in history (or training data). However, it is not feasible to have a long l which imposes unnecessary complexity during the on-line recommendation process. For this reason, only the last visited k pages are used for probability calculation in Eq. 3.22 where $k \ll l$ identifies the order of the Markov model. After calculating the Markov parameters of each cluster, the active user session is assigned to the cluster that maximizes the probability in Eq. 3.17. Then the recommendation set is generated using the transition matrix of that cluster.

Another way is to represent each cluster of user sessions by a tree, which is called Click-Stream Tree (CST) [Gündüz-Ögüdücü and Özsu, 2006]. Each user session in a cluster is a branch of the corresponding CST. Each CST has a *root* node, which is labeled as "null". Each node, except the *root* node, consists of three fields: *data*, *count* and *next_node*. *Data* field consists of page information. *Count* field registers the number of sessions represented by the portion of the path arriving at that node. *Next_node* links to the next node in the CST that has the same *data* field or null if there is any node with the same *data* field. Each CST has a *data_table*, which consists of two fields: *data* field and *first_node* that links to the first node in the CST that has the *data* field. The children of each node in the click-stream tree is ordered in the count-descending order such that a child node with bigger count is closer to its parent node. The resulting click-stream trees are then used for recommendation.

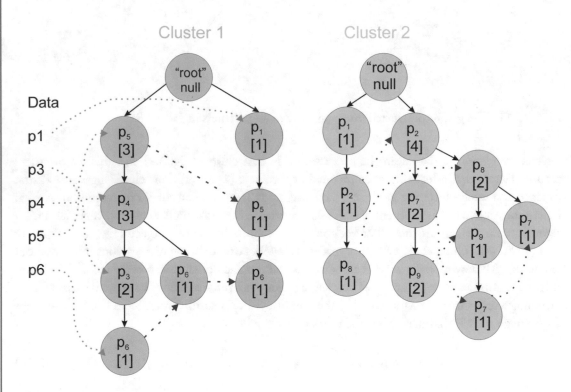

Figure 3.12: Click stream treas of two clusters for user sessions in Table 3.3

Example 4 Let's illustrate the construction of CST with an example. Let the sessions in Table 3.3 be clustered into 2 clusters as in Fig 3.11. Fig. 3.12 shows the constructed CSTs of these clusters. Circles represent tree nodes. Each node in a tree has a *data* field and a *count* field (shown in Fig. 3.12 as [count] in the second line in each node). For simplicity, only the *data_table* of the first cluster is presented.

When a request is received from an active user, a recommendation set consisting of k different pages that the user has not yet visited, is produced using the best matching user session[2]. For the first two requests of an active user session, all clusters are explored to find the one that best matches the active user session. After the second request of the active user, top-N clusters that have higher recommendation scores among other clusters are selected for producing further recommendation sets. The recommendation score of a cluster is defined as the similarity value between the active user session, and the best matching session resides in that cluster. For the remaining requests, the best matching user session is found by exploring the top-N clusters that have the highest N similarity values computed using the first two requests of the active user session. The rest of the recommendations for the same active user session are made by using the top-N clusters.

3.5 COMBINATION OF WEB PAGE RECOMMENDER SYSTEMS

Recommender systems have been extensively explored in Web mining. However, the quality of recommendations and the user satisfaction with such systems are still not optimal. Since different methods describe different characteristics of Web users, they produce different prediction accuracies on the same data set. Combination of different methods may result in better accuracy. For example, consider two different Web users surfing on the same Web site and two different recommender models applied to this Web site to predict three pages one of which could be the next request of a Web user. Suppose two users, user 1 and user 2, are navigating through a Web site. Let model A and model B be two different recommendation models employed on the site. The last page requests of user 1 and user 2 are pages p_1 and p_4, respectively, where p_i is a Web page on the Web site. Before the last page requests of users, based on the navigating pages of users model A generates a recommendation set $RS_A = \{p_1, p_2, p_3\}$ for both users while model B generates $RS_B = \{p_2, p_4, p_5\}$. In this case, model A is successful for user 1 and model B is successful for user 2. However, if it is possible to combine these two models into one model to generate a single recommendation set, for example, such that $RS = \{p_1, p_4, p_5\}$, this combined model can generate correct recommendations for both of the users.

Recommender systems based on Web mining techniques have also strengths and weaknesses [Kazienko and Kolodziejski, 2006]. Therefore, the need for hybrid approaches, that combine the benefits of multiple algorithms has been discussed [Burke, 2002]. The main idea behind the hybrid models is to exploit the advantages of different approaches while avoiding their shortcomings. Hybrid recommender systems combine two or more techniques to improve recommender performance. In his paper Burke [2002], implemented hybrid recommenders for collaborative filtering that combine information across different sources. To date, most of the research on hybrid recommenders is on collaborative filtering approaches such as combining these approaches with content based approaches rather than combining multiple recommender techniques. The performance of a

---

[2]The user session that has the highest similarity to the active user session is defined as the best matching session.

recommender model depends on several factors besides its technique: on the structure of the Web site and on Web users. Thus, it could be difficult to estimate a single best model for recommendation.

In one of the early studies, a framework was designed to combine three major recommendation approaches including content based (using the product attributes), demographic filtering (using the customer attributes) and CF techniques [Pazzani, 1999]. Furthermore, hybrid approaches that utilize content information are proposed by Burke [2002] to overcome some of the shortcomings of CF such as the cold start problems for new users and new products. In this work, six different hybridization methods are surveyed and implemented. Most of the work in this area is concerned with combining content, structure and usage information to generate hybrid systems. In recent years, there has been an increasing interest in applying Web content mining techniques to build Web recommender systems. However, the Web content mining techniques are unable to handle constantly changing Web sites, such as news sites, and dynamically created Web pages. Thus, using Web content mining techniques in a recommender model leads to updating the model frequently. Independent from the data used in different recommender systems, in this chapter, we discussed how to combine these recommender systems. The aim of a hybrid recommender system is to combine multiple recommender techniques or to combine multiple results of different recommender models together to produce a single output.

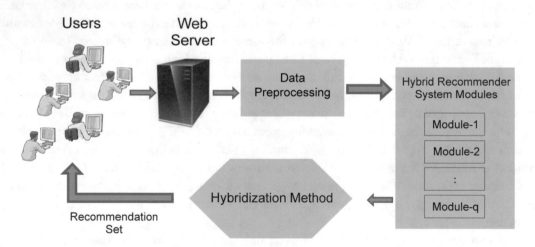

Figure 3.13: A sample hybrid recommender system

A hybrid recommender system combines different recommendation models, which are called modules of the hybrid as shown in Fig. 3.13. The modules may differ in the knowledge or in the technique they use to build the model. For example, a content based model and a usage based model may be combined in order to handle the cold-start problem. Alternatively, different recommender models, which are based on the same data source but use different techniques, can also be combined. Given a user's current request for each of the modules the hybrid generates, in parallel, a candidate recommendation set (RS_i), consisting of k pages it thinks the user will visit as the next page in her session. The hybrid recommender integrates the individual recommendation sets using one of the integration methods and generates a final recommendation set (RS) with k pages as well:

$$RS = RS_1 \circ RS_2 \circ \ldots \circ RS_q \tag{3.23}$$

where "$\circ$" denotes the integration method. Burke [2002] introduces six different types of hybridization methods. In this section, these methods will be explained briefly.

3.5.1   COMBINATION METHODS

Weighted: A weighted Web recommender is the simplest design of hybrid recommenders in which each module of the hybrid scores a given item based on the item ratings or weights [Burke, 2002]. After each component generates a candidate set the union or the intersect of the candidate sets is used as the final candidate set. Each component scores the items in the final candidate set, and the linear combination of the computed scores becomes the item's prediction rate.

In Web page recommendation, items correspond to Web pages; thus, each individual recommendation set is defined by a tuple:

$$RS_i = (PAGES_i, \ WEIGHTS_i)$$

where $PAGES_i$ is a subset of the pages on the Web site, $\mathcal{P} = \{p_1, ..., p_N\}$, that the $module_i$ generates as a recommendation set, and $WEIGHTS_i$ is the associated weights of pages in $PAGES_i$:

$$PAGES_i = \{p_1^i, ..., p_k^i\}$$

$$WEIGHTS_i = \{weight_{p_1^i}, ..., weight_{p_k^i}\}$$

where $p_j^i = p_l$ for some $l \in \{1, \ldots, N\}$, and $weight_{p_j}$ is the weight of page p_j if $p_j \in PAGES_i$. The hybrid recommender then generates the combined recommendation set ($CRS = (PAGES, \ WEIGHTS)$) where $PAGES$ is the union of $PAGES_i$ for $i = \{1, \ldots, q\}$ and $WEIGTHS$ is the combined recommendation scores. The combined recommendation score of a page p_i is calculated by summing up the weights of this page in each recommendation set. The pages in CRS are then sorted by the combined recommendation score and the top k pages shown to the user as the final recommendation set RS.

Mixed: A mixed hybrid presents recommendations from more than one technique together [Burke, 2002]. However, the challenge of these types of hybrids is one of the integration of ranked pages in each recommendation set into a final recommendation set. Three methods are proposed to remedy this problem [Göksedef and Gündüz-Ögüdücü, 2010]. Initially, equal weights (m_i) are assigned to each module of the hybrid, assuming that each module generates equally accurate recommendations. Each module of the hybrid generates a recommendation set consisting of k pages.

$$RS_i = \{p_1^i, p_2^i, \ldots, p_k^i\} \tag{3.24}$$

where $p_j^i = p_l$ for some $l \in \{1, \ldots, N\}$. Then the individual recommendation sets are combined to get a final recommendation set, which consists of k pages also, as follows:

$$RS = \{p_i | p_i \in RS_1 \ and \ i = 1, .., m_1\}$$
$$\cup \ldots \cup \{p_j | p_j \in RS_q \ and \ j = 1, .., m_q\}$$

where $m_1, \ldots, m_q \in \{0, 1, 2, \ldots, k-1\}$ and $\sum_i m_i = k$ and $p_0 = \emptyset$. Note that each module has m_i pages in the final recommendation set and at least two of the modules contribute to the final recommendation set. After each recommendation, the weights of the modules are updated by evaluating their performance. Three different methods can be used to update these weights [Göksedef and Gündüz-Ögüdücü, 2010], according to the utility as defined in Section 2.5:

Method 1.   Find best and worst modules according to the utility they provide in the last user session.

Method 2.   Find best and worst modules according to the utility they provide for the first two pages in the active user session.

Method 3.   Find best and worst modules according to the utility they provide until the current user session.

In all of the three methods, the weight of the best module is increased whereas the weight of the worst module is decreased, considering minimum and maximum weight values of the modules.

Switching: The switching criterion is used to decide when to switch between the different used modules.

The switching hybrid selects one of its modules as appropriate in the current situation based on its switching criterion. The idea behind this is that the modules may have not consistent performance for all types of users. Each of the modules generates its individual recommendation set as in Eq. 3.24. Then, the switching hybrid selects one of the individual recommendation sets as the final recommendation set, namely $RS = RS_i$, based on its switching criterion. However, a switching hybrid requires a reliable switching criterion based on either the performance of the individual recommenders or some alternative measure. The disadvantage of switching hybrids is that the parameterization needed for determining the switching criterion is complex.

Feature Combination: The idea of feature combination is to merge the features of different data sources and associate them with each item to be recommended. For example, collaborative information can be treated as additional features associated with each Web page, and content based techniques can be used in the typical way on augmented dataset. This kind of hybrid is not a "real" hybrid in the sense that it combines multiple recommender models. There is only one recommendation model that generated the recommendation set, but it works on a data set in which new kinds of features are added to the items. The reason to call it hybrid is that it uses different knowledge sources.

Feature Augmentation: Feature augmentation method is similar in some ways to the feature combination method. However, instead of merging multiple sets of features, a feature augmentation hybrid involves a staged process. In the first stage, new features are generated for each item by using one of the contributing recommendation models of the hybrid. Afterwards, a second recommendation model, called the primary recommendation model, takes the obtained features and incorporates into its recommendation process. For example, association rule mining can be applied over the collaborative data to derive new content features for content-based recommendation. Usually, two different recommender models contribute to the feature augmented hybrid. It is suggested to use a feature augmentation recommender when there is a well-developed strong primary recommendation component and a desire to add additional knowledge sources [Burke, 2002]. The advantage of feature augmentation hybrid over the feature combination one is that it adds a smaller number of features to the primary recommender's input in order to improve the performance of the primary recommender.

Cascade: Due to its hierarchical structure, the cascade hybrid is similar to the feature augmentation hybrid. But in these systems, all of the modules of the hybrid preserve their function in providing predicted ratings. These systems also involve a staged process. A recommendation model produces first a coarse ranking of candidates. Afterwards, a subsequent recommendation technique uses the previous filtered candidate set, refining the final suggestions.

Meta-Level: These systems involve a staged process where they use a model learned by one recommender as input for another. The actual recommender does not work with any raw profile data. Instead of its original knowledge source, the actual recommender uses in its computation a learned model, which is replaced completely by the contributing recommender. Unfortunately, it is not always straightforward to derive a meta-level hybrid from any given pair of recommenders since the contributing recommender has to produce some kind of model that can be used as input by the actual recommender which is not feasible for all recommendation techniques.

Some of these hybridization methods are applied for Web page prediction [Göksedef and Gündüz-Ögüdücü, 2010; Jin et al., 2005; Khalil et al., 2006; Li and Zaïane, 2004], and it is found that hybrid recommender systems improve the recommendation accuracy. However, if the hybridization method is wrongly chosen, then the performance of the hybrid can also be lower than its components. For this reason, it is particularly important to examine the performance of each module of the hybrid on the data set. In some hybrids, such as weighted, mixed or switching, the individual performance of the modules should be taken into consideration when choosing a recommender model as a module of the hybrid. Another important issue is not to increase the time unacceptably to generate recommendations in the on-line step. For this reason, different recommendation models can be combined in the off-line phase. A rule based approach is also proposed to minimize Web site administration overhead and quickly adapt to changing situations [Thor and Rahm, 2004].

3.6   SEMANTIC WEB

In Web page recommendation, the goal is the development of an effective prediction algorithm. The core issue in prediction is the development of an effective algorithm that deduces the future user requests. The most successful approach towards this goal has been the exploitation of the user's access history to derive prediction. An active research area is to combine the domain knowledge with the Web mining process, i.e., approaches based on semantic Web mining techniques. Semantic Web is defined by Berners-Lee et al. [2001] as "an extension of the current Web in which information is given well-defined meaning, better enabling computers and people to work in cooperation". Most of the today's Web content is designed for human consumption. A user, who needs information that is spread over various documents, must identify these documents through several queries. Even if a Web page recommender system helps the user identify relevant documents, it is the person who must extract the partial information from them and put it together which is a very time-consuming activity. Search engines and Web page recommendation models help users locate the relevant documents but they do not support in retrieving information from them. At present, the main obstacle to providing better support to Web users is that the meaning of Web content is not suitable for effectively processing by computers.

HTML is a standard language in which Web pages is written. There are tools to parse them in order to extract text to be indexed. When this information is used in a Web page recommendation model, it enables to retrieve relevant Web pages. But, it is not sufficient to interpret the meaning of these pages to satisfy users' needs. Let us consider a simple example. A Web site of a sport centre offers possibilities to various sport activities. A portion of a typical Web page of this site might look like this:

```
<h1>Oceanic Sport Centre</h1>
Welcome to the home page of the Oceanic Pilates studio. If you
want a break from treadmills, weight rooms, or the pool, why
not consider Pilates? Oceanic Sport Centre instructors bring
specialized skills that enhance your Pilates experience, whatever
your current level of fitness.


<h2>Class hours</h2>
Monday - 9:30 am (Advanced Class)<br>
Monday - 5:30 pm<br>
Wednesday - 9:30 am (Advanced Class)<br>
Wednesday - 5:30 pm<br>
Friday - 9:30 am<br>
We do not offer private lessons during
<a href="…"> Yoga </a> lessons.
```

A recommender system which utilizes content data will identify the word "pool" and may recommend this page to Web users, who are determined by the system as being interested in swimming. Such a Web page may be suitable for Web site users who are looking information about Pilates lessons. But, even these users should read the page and find the exact class hours or follow the link to the Yoga class to find the schedule of private lessons.

The semantic Web approach for Web page recommendation proposes to attack this problem by mapping the content of a Web site into an ontology. Following Antoniou and van Harmelen [2008], an ontology is "an explicit of a shared understanding of a conceptualization". Domain-specific ontologies are considered as one of the pillars of semantic Web, which include a set of concepts, a hierarchy on them, and relations between concepts. For example, for a university Web site, staff members, students, courses, departments, projects are some concepts. A relationship, which includes hierarchies of classes, specifies that a sub-concept C inherits all properties and relationships from its super-concept C'. For example, all faculty are staff members. The semantic relations defined in the ontologies provide the recommendation systems with the capability to infer related knowledge from Web content.

The aim of Web page recommender systems based on semantic Web mining techniques is to identify users' needs and to relate these needs and the content of Web pages in order to produce enhanced recommendations. In most of these systems, the meta-data is exploited in the form of ontologies, which describe the content of Web pages and user profiles in a general way. Figure 3.14 depicts how a recommendation system based on semantic Web mining techniques works. Like many other recommendation models, Web server logs and Web page content can be used as data sources. It is necessary to build first a domain ontology for the Web site. However, creating ontologies from Web sites is a difficult task that involves specialists from several fields, including domain modelers and knowledge engineers. The ontology is comprised of the thematic categories covered by the Web pages of the Web site which makes the Web site ontology strongly related to the site's topology. The Web pages are instances of one or more concepts. These concepts are linked by relationships, such as "is-a" or "has part". However, some concepts and their relations can only be extracted by examining the inter-page structure, especially for the case that the descriptive information of one concept is distributed across multiple pages. Since the construction of an ontology is out of the scope of this manuscript, it is assumed that an ontology is built semi-automatically or manually for the Web site.

To provide semantic Web page recommendations, user interaction on a Web page can also be tracked on an event basis, enhanced with semantic knowledge to understand the user intention [Zhou et al., 2005]. A day is divided into 6 activity periods called *real-life time concepts*: *Early Morning, Morning, Noon, Early Afternoon, Late Afternoon, Evening* and *Night*. A set of unique event attributes such as *Games, Adults, Sports* and *Entertainment* are defined to describe Web access activities. Each Web page in each user session is mapped one of the event attributes and associated with one of the real-life time concepts according to time of the Web page being accessed. These two kinds of knowledge in the mapped users sessions are then used to construct an ontology called *usage*

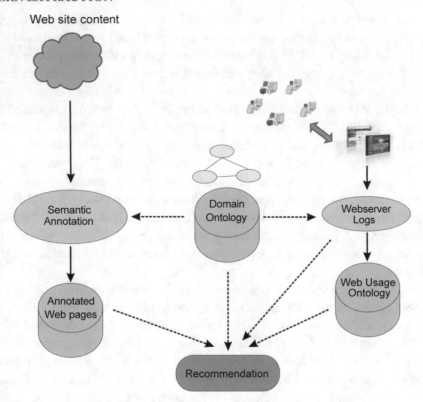

Figure 3.14: Process of a recommendation system based on semantic Web mining

ontology. For example, a ranked list of Web content categories that are most relevant to the user's interests for a specific time interval can be obtained from usage ontology.

Once user sessions are mapped to concepts in domain ontology or in usage ontology, data mining approaches are applied to gain knowledge from these transformed data. These approaches in subsequent mining steps operate on concepts at a chosen level of abstraction. For example, association rules can be generated like "visitors who are interests in *projects* may also be interested in *publications*". Alternatively, activity rules can be obtained such as "75% of visitors who visit the site between [19 : 00 : 00, 20 : 00 : 00] tend do read Web content related to *sports*". Applying clustering methods to sets of sessions, related concepts can be identified at different levels of abstraction.

It is difficult to generate recommendations at the Web page level when using semantic Web mining techniques. However, these techniques have advantage in sites with dynamically generated Web pages, where each individual page will be requested so infrequently that no regularities may be found in an analysis of navigation behavior on Web page level. Rather, regularities may exist at a more abstract level. Second, semantic Web mining techniques for recommendation may solve the cold-start problem when new pages are added to the Web site. A course Web page p, newly introduced into a faculty Web site structure, cannot be recommended simply because it was not in the site before and thus could not occur in any user sessions. A knowledge of regularities at a more abstract level could help to derive a recommendation of p because it deals with the Topic "Data Mining" (and there are criteria for recommending courses on that Topic). However, the main obstacle for applying semantic Web mining techniques for recommendation is that building ontologies for many domains is quite labor-intensive and demands high level of proficiency of expert. Besides, the recommendation techniques are also domain dependent due to the use of domain ontologies.

CHAPTER 4

Evaluation Metrics

Most of the work for evaluating recommender models are conducted for collaborative filtering recommenders where user ratings of items are available. However, the aim of every recommendation model is to increase the recommendation accuracy. Thus, when dealing with Web page prediction, much of the evaluation work has focused on accuracy. The evaluation process is usually performed off-line. In this case, the entire data set is separated randomly as training and test sets. Alternatively, the data set can be partitioned into training and test sets according to time periods. The model is built using the training set whereas the accuracy results are given on test set.

The calculation of accuracy differs based on the generation of recommendation set. Assume that the model generates a recommendation set $\mathcal{R}(s_{ij})$ consisting of k pages given the first j pages of a user session s_i in the test set. A hit is declared if any one of the k recommended pages is the next request of the user. The *hit-ratio* [Gündüz-Ögüdücü and Özsu, 2006] (or *click-through* [Cosley et al., 2002]) is the number of hits obtained in the test set divided by the total number of recommendations made by the system.

The accuracy of a recommender model can be evaluated in terms of *precision* and *coverage* metrics [Li and Zaïane, 2004; Mobasher et al., 2001c]. For simplicity, suppose that the weights of Web pages in Eq. 2.6 are equal to one. A user session of length l can be represented as $s_i = \langle p_1^i, p_2^i, \ldots, p_l^i \rangle$. The precision of the model is defined as:

$$Precision = \frac{\sum_{s_i} \frac{|\cup_{p_j^i} T(s_{ij}) \cap \mathcal{R}(s_{ij})|}{|\cup_{p_j^i} \mathcal{R}(s_{ij})|}}{|\mathcal{S}_t|} \qquad (4.1)$$

where $T(s_{ij}) = (p_{j+1}^i, \ldots, p_l^i)$ is the remaining portion of s_i used to evaluate the generated recommendations and $|\mathcal{S}_t|$ is the number of user sessions in the test set. Coverage is defined as:

$$Coverage = \frac{\sum_{s_i} \frac{|\cup_{p_j^i} (T(s_{ij}) \cap \mathcal{R}(s_{ij})|}{|\cup_{p_j^i} T(s_{ij})|}}{|\mathcal{S}_t|} \qquad (4.2)$$

Precision measures the degree to which the recommendation model produces accurate recommendations whereas coverage measures the ability of the recommendation model to produce all of the pages that are likely to be visited by the user.

Selecting appropriate evaluation metrics depends on several parameters, such as which users' utility the model was designed for or whether the comparison of the chosen metric is comparable to other published research work in the literature or not. For example, the hit-ratio metric is not appropriate to evaluate the performance of a recommendation model based on association rule mining. Since these kinds of recommender models do not consider the order of page requests, they may yield to a low hit-ratio value whereas the precision and coverage values of these models may be higher. However, at this point, another question arises: How large should the difference be in the values of evaluation metrics in order to consider it statistically significant? It is difficult to give an exact answer to this question. For example, the Netflix Prize was awarded on September 2009 to a team for a 10% improvement of the accuracy of the service's recommendation. When examining the literature on the recommendation algorithms, it can be concluded that many researchers find that their newest algorithms yield a better performance.

However, accuracy is not a complete indicator of the performance of a recommender model. New metrics called *recommendation diversity* and *popularity* are proposed [Zhou et al., 2010] to evaluate recommender models based on collaborative filtering techniques where user specific recommendations are generated. When evaluating a recommender algorithm in the context of the *Find Good Items* task where items, that are unlikely to be discovered by users themselves, are desired, diversity and novelty should be taken into consideration. It is stated that accurate recommendations evaluated off-line are not always useful. If an algorithm does not make the recommendations to a single user diverse enough, users may get tired of receiving many recommended objects under the same topic. Recommender models, based on the similarity of users, may be unable to recommend items that a user might like, but would never find on her own. It is desirable to design a model that provides the diversity of recommendations; namely, different users should be recommended for different items. The diversity of two recommendation sets are measured by Hamming distance that tells how different the items are in these sets. Fig. 4 illustrates these situations.

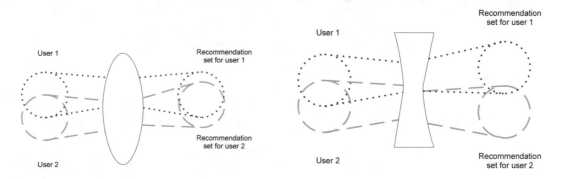

Figure 4.1: Generation of similarity-focused and diversity-focused recommendations

It is an important issue to evaluate the off-line effectiveness of a recommender model (as is done in many research papers) rather than the actual recommendations for real users. A high recommendation accuracy in off-line evaluation will not give users of recommender systems an effective and satisfying experience since this high accuracy value is achieved by only recommending popular items, which are easy to predict. Moreover, it is not necessary to employ a recommender model to predict those items. There is an important issue here: a system that recommends page p for user u will be rewarded if in the test data user u did indeed visit that page. However, it is entirely possible that the user would have visited the page anyway, since it is a hub page. The point is summarized in [Zhang and Iyengar, 2002]:

> the true value of a recommender system can only be measured by controlled experiments with actual users. Such an experiment could measure the improvement achieved by a specific recommendation algorithm when compared to, say, recommending the most popular item. Experiments with historical data have been used to estimate the value of recommender algorithms in the absence of controlled live experiments…

Besides accuracy and usefulness of the recommendation results, it is important to generate recommendations in an acceptable time period during the on-line recommendation phase. The processes of extracting user profile and preparing other data such as content of the Web site are conducted off-line. However, with many users and a high number of Web pages, these tasks are computationally very expensive and time consuming. Some of the recommender models are very effective in providing recommendations for a user that visits a given Web site. However, it has been widely remarked that their performances significantly decrease in other Web sites that have a high number of users or Web pages in the Web site. Besides the number of Web pages, another important parameter is the number of features considered in the user's profile for each Web page that a user visits. It is important that methods for generating recommendations from the extracted users' profiles ought to be fast enough to make online recommendation possible. Thus, the time complexity of model building and recommendation generation is an important evaluation parameter of the real-time recommendation system.

It is now common for users to navigate the Web using mobile devices such as smart phones. These mobile devices present limited Internet connections and display capabilities, which make users demand a light site presentation without large sized graphical objects. For this reason, a recommendation model should consider users' contextual information and integrate it into the model to provide adaptive recommendations to mitigate potential environmental impacts.

Unfortunately, there is not a single recommender model that achieves all these goals. Every model has weaknesses and strengths. The selection of an appropriate model for a specific task is therefore essential to obtain reliable results.

Bibliography

R. C. Agarwal, C. C. Aggarwal, and V. V. V. Prasad. A Tree Projection Algorithm For Generation of Frequent Itemsets. *J. Parall. and Distrib. Comput.*, 61(3):350–371, 2001. DOI: 10.1006/jpdc.2000.1693 37

C. C. Aggarwal, J. L. Wolf, K. Wu, and P. S. Yu. Horting Hatches an Egg: A New Graph-Theoretic Approach to Collaborative Filtering. In *Proc. 5th ACM SIGKDD Int. Conf. on Knowledge Discovery and Data Mining*, pages 201–212, 1999. DOI: 10.1145/312129.312230 9

R. Agrawal and R. Srikant. Mining Sequential Patterns. In *Proc. 11th Int. Conf. on Data Engineering*, pages 3–14, 1995. DOI: 10.1109/ICDE.1995.380415 45

R. Agrawal, T. Imielinski, and A. Swami. Mining Association Rules between Sets of Items in Large Databases. In *Proc. of the ACM SIGMOD Conf. on Management of Data*, pages 207–216, 1993. DOI: 10.1145/170036.170072 35

D. J. Aldous. Reorganizing Large Web Sites. *Amer. Math. Monthly*, 108:16–27, 2001. DOI: 10.2307/2695672 3

M. Altheim and S. McCarron. XHTML™ 1.0: The Extensible Hypertext Markup Language (Second Edition), 2001. URL http://www.w3.org/TR/xhtml1/. 6

G. Antoniou and F. van Harmelen. *A Semantic Web Primer*. MIT Press, 2 edition, 2008. 61

R. A. Baeza-Yates and B. Ribeiro-Neto. *Modern Information Retrieval*. Addison-Wesley Longman Publishing Co., Inc., 1999. 34

M. Balabanović and Y. Shoham. Fab: Content-Based, Collaborative Recommendation. *Commun. ACM*, 40(3):66–72, 1997. DOI: 10.1145/245108.245124 34

P. Baldi, P. Frasconi, and P. Smyth. *Modeling the Internet and the Web: Probabilstic Methods and Algorithms*. Wiley, 2003. 22, 46

A. Banerjee and J. Ghosh. Clickstream Clustering using Weighted Longest Common Subsequences. In *Proc. of the Web Mining Workshop at the 1st SIAM Conf. on Data Mining*, pages 33–40, 2001. 49, 50, 52

T. Berners-Lee, J. Hendler, and O. Lassila. The Semantic Web. *Scientific American*, 284(5):34–43, 2001. DOI: 10.1038/scientificamerican0501-34 60

A. Bestavros. Using Speculation to Reduce Server Load and Service Time on the WWW. In *Proc. 4th Int. Conf. on Information and Knowledge Management*, pages 403–410, 1995. DOI: 10.1145/221270.221653 46

J. Borges and M. Levene. Data Mining of User Navigation Patterns. In *Proc. Int. Workshop WEBKDD99 – Web Usage Analysis and User Profiling*, pages 31–36, 1999. DOI: 10.1007/3-540-44934-5_6 1, 46

R. Burke. Hybrid Recommender Systems: Survey and Experiments. *User Modeling and User-Adapted Interaction*, 12(4):331–370, 2002. DOI: 10.1023/A:1021240730564 43, 55, 56, 57, 59

I. Cadez, D. Heckerman, C. Meek, P. Smyth, and S. White. Model-Based Clustering and Visualization of Navigation Patterns on a Web Site. *Data Min. Knowl. Discov.*, 7(4):399–424, 2003. DOI: 10.1023/A:1024992613384 48, 49

L. D. Catledge and J. E. Pitkow. Characterizing Browsing Behaviors on the World Wide Web. Technical Report GIT-GVU-95-13, Georgia Institute of Technology, 1995. 17

S. Chakrabarti. Data Mining for Hypertext: A Tutorial Survey. *ACM SIGKDD Explor. Newsl.*, 1 (2):1–11, 2000. DOI: 10.1145/846183.846187 5, 22

R. Cooley, B. Mobasher, and J. Srivastava. Data Preparation for Mining World Wide Web Browsing Patterns. *Knowl. and Information Syst.*, 1(1):5–32, 1999. 13, 19

D. Cosley, S. Lawrence, and D. M. Pennock. REFEREE: An Open Framework for Practical Testing of Recommender Systems using Researchindex. In *Proc. 28th Int. Conf. on Very Large Data Bases*, pages 35–46, 2002. DOI: 10.1016/B978-155860869-6/50012-3 65

G. N. Demir, Ş. Uyar, and Ş. Gündüz-Ögüdücü. Multiobjective Evolutionary Clustering of Web User Sessions: A Case Study in Web Page Recommendation. *Soft Comput.*, 14(6):579–597, 2010. DOI: 10.1007/s00500-009-0428-y 53

A.P. Dempster, N.M. Laird, and D.B. Rubin. Maximum Likelihood from Incomplete Data via the EM Algorithm. *J. Royal Statistical Society, Series B*, 39(1):1–38, 1977. 48

M. Deshpande and G. Karypis. Item-Based Top-N Recommendation Algorithms. *ACM Trans. Information Syst.*, 22(1):143–177, 2004. DOI: 10.1145/963770.963776 33

A. Driga, P. Lu, J. Schaeffer, D. Szafron, K. Charter, and I. Parsons. FastLSA: A Fast, Linear-Space, Parallel and Sequential Algorithm for Sequence Alignment. *Algorithmica*, 45(3):337–375, 2006. DOI: 10.1007/s00453-006-1217-y 50

H. A. Edelstein. Pan for Gold in the Clickstream. Information Week, March 2001. 20

O. Etzioni. The World Wide Web: Quagmire or Gold Mine. *Commun. ACM*, 39(11):65–68, 1996. DOI: 10.1145/240455.240473 1

R. Forsati and M. R. Meybodi. Effective Page Recommendation Algorithms Based on Distributed Learning Automata and Weighted Association Rules. *Expert Syst. Appl.*, 37(2):1316–1330, 2010. DOI: 10.1016/j.eswa.2009.06.010 36

A. Foss, W. Wang, and O. R. Zaïane. A Non-Parametric Approach to Web Log Analysis. In *Proc. of the Web Mining Workshop at the 1st SIAM Conf. on Data Mining*, pages 41–50, 2001. 53

A. Gediminas and T. Alexander. Toward the Next Generation of Recommender Systems: A Survey of the State-of-the-Art and Possible Extensions. *IEEE Trans. Knowl. and Data Eng.*, 17(6): 734–749, 2005. DOI: 10.1109/TKDE.2005.99 22

M. Girvan and M. E. J. Newman. Community Structure in Social and Biological Networks. *Proc. of the National Academy of Sciences of the United States of America*, 99(3):7821–7826, 2002. DOI: 10.1073/pnas.122653799 41

E. J. Glover, K. Tsioutsiouliklis, S. Lawrence, D. M. Pennock, and G. W. Flake. Using Web Structure for Classifying and Describing Web Pages. In *Proc. 11th Int. World Wide Web Conf.*, pages 562–569, 2002. DOI: 10.1145/511446.511520 39

M. Göksedef and S. Gündüz-Ögüdücü. A Consensus Recommender for Web Users. In *Proc. of the 3rd Int. Conf. on Advance Data Mining and Applications*, pages 287–299, 2007. DOI: 10.1007/978-3-540-73871-8_27 49

M. Göksedef and S. Gündüz-Ögüdücü. Combination of Web Page Recommender Systems. *Expert Syst. Appl.*, 37(4):2911–2922, 2010. DOI: 10.1016/j.eswa.2009.09.046 52, 57, 58, 59

D. Goldberg, D. Nichols, B. Oki, and D. Terry. Using Collaborative Filtering to Weave an Information Tapestry. *Commun. ACM*, 35(12):61–70, 1992. DOI: 10.1145/138859.138867 1, 27

S. Guha, R. Rastogi, and K. Shim. ROCK: A Robust Clustering Algorithm for Categorical Attributes. In *Proc. 15th Int. Conf. on Data Engineering*, page 512, 1999. DOI: 10.1109/ICDE.1999.754967 53

S. Gündüz-Ögüdücü and M. T. Özsu. Incremental Click-Stream Tree Model: Learning from New Users for Web Page Prediction. *Distrib. Parall. Databases*, 19(1):5–27, 2006. DOI: 10.1007/s10619-006-6284-1 49, 51, 52, 53, 65

J. Han and M. Kamber. *Data Mining: Concepts and Techniques*. Morgan Kaufmann Publishers Inc., 2 edition, 2006. 2, 38

J. Han, J. Pei, and Y. Yin. Mining Frequent Patterns without Candidate Generation. *ACM SIGMOD Rec.*, 29(2):1–12, 2000. DOI: 10.1145/335191.335372 35

J. L. Herlocker, J. A. Konstan, L. G. Terveen, and J. T. Riedl. Evaluating Collaborative Filtering Recommender Systems. *ACM Trans. Information Syst.*, 22(1):5–53, 2004. DOI: 10.1145/963770.963772 28

J. Hipp, U. Güntzer, and G. Nakhaeizadeh. Algorithms for Association Rule Mining — A General Survey and Comparison. *ACM SIGKDD Explor. Newsl.*, 2(1):58–64, 2000. DOI: 10.1145/360402.360421 36

J. Hou and Y. Zhang. Constructing Good Quality Web Page Communities. In *Proc. 13th Australasian Database Conf.*, pages 65–74, 2002. DOI: 10.1145/563932.563914 2

J. Hou and Y. Zhang. Effectively Finding Relevant Web Pages from Linkage Information. *IEEE Trans. Knowl. and Data Eng.*, 15(4):940–951, 2003. DOI: 10.1109/TKDE.2003.1209010 2

C. Hsu and M. Dung. Generating Finite-State Transducers for Semi-Structured Data Extraction from the Web. *Inf. Syst.*, 23(9):521–538, 1998. DOI: 10.1016/S0306-4379(98)00027-1 21

X. Huang, A. An, N. Cercone, and G. Promhouse. Discovery of Interesting Association Rules from Livelink Web Log Data. In *Proc. 2002 IEEE Int. Conf. on Data Mining*, page 763, 2002. DOI: 10.1109/ICDM.2002.1184048 36

W. Jicheng, H. Yuan, W. Gangshan, and Z. Fuyan. Web Mining: Knowledge Discovery on the Web. In *Systems, Man, and Cybernetics, 1999 IEEE International Conf.*, pages 137–141, 1999. DOI: 10.1109/ICSMC.1999.825222 2

X. Jin, Y. Zhou, and B. Mobasher. A Maximum Entropy Web Recommendation System: Combining Collaborative and Content Features. In *Proc. 11th ACM SIGKDD Int. Conf. on Knowledge Discovery and Data Mining*, pages 612–617, 2005. DOI: 10.1145/1081870.1081945 59

G. Karypis, E. (S.) Han, and V. Kumar. Chameleon: Hierarchical Clustering Using Dynamic Modeling. *Comput.*, 32(8):68–75, 1999. DOI: 10.1109/2.781637 53

P. Kazienko and P. Kolodziejski. Personalized Integration of Recommendation Methods for E-commerce. *J. of Comp. Sci. and Appl.*, 3(3):12–26, 2006. 55

F. Khalil, J. Li, and H. Wang. A Framework of Combining Markov Model with Association Rules for Predicting Web Page Accesses. In *Proc. of the 5th Australasian Conf. on Data mining and Analytics*, pages 177–184, 2006. 59

F. Khalil, J. Li, and H. Wang. Integrating Recommendation Models for Improved Web Page Prediction accuracy. In *Proc. of the 31st Australasian Conf. on Computer Science*, pages 91–100, 2008. 45

J. M. Kleinberg. Authoritative Sources in a Hyperlinked Environment. *J. ACM*, 46(5):604–632, 1999. DOI: 10.1145/324133.324140 2

J. A. Konstan, B. N. Miller, D. Maltz, J. L. Herlocker, L. R. Gordon, and J. Riedl. Grouplens: Applying Collaborative Filtering to Usenet News. *Commun. ACM*, 40(3):77–87, 1997. DOI: 10.1145/245108.245126 30

R. Kosala and H. Blockeel. Web Mining Research: A Survey. *ACM SIGKDD Explor. Newsl.*, 2(1): 1–15, 2000. DOI: 10.1145/360402.360406 5

M. Koster. A Method for Web Robots Control. Internet Draft, The Internet Engineering Task Force (IETF), 1996. URL http://www.robotstxt.org/norobots-rfc.txt. 15

N. Kushmerick. *Wrapper induction for information extraction*. PhD thesis, Washington, 1997. 21

J. Li and O. R. Zaïane. Combining Usage, Content, and Structure Data to Improve Web Site Recommendation. In *Proc. 5th Int. Conf. on Electronic Commerce and Web Technologies*, pages 305–315, 2004. DOI: 10.1007/978-3-540-30077-9_31 59, 65

G. Linden, B. Smith, and J. York. Amazon.com Recommendations: Item-to-Item Collaborative Filtering. *IEEE Internet Comput.*, 7(1):76–80, 2003. DOI: 10.1109/MIC.2003.1167344 32, 33

B. Liu, W. Hsu, and Y. Ma. Mining Association Rules with Multiple Minimum Supports. In *Proc. 5th ACM SIGKDD Int. Conf. on Knowledge Discovery and Data Mining*, pages 337–341, 1999. DOI: 10.1145/312129.312274 36

S. K. Madria, S. S. Bhowmick, W. K. Ng, and E. P. Lim. Research Issues in Web Data Mining. In *Proc. 1st Int. Conf. Data Warehousing and Knowledge Discovery*, pages 303–312, 1999. DOI: 10.1007/3-540-48298-9_32 2

B. Mobasher, H. Dai, T. Luo, Y. Sun, and J. Zhu. Integrating Web Usage and Content Mining for More Effective Personalization. In *Proc. 1st Int. Conf. on Electronic and Web Technologies*, pages 165–176, 2000. DOI: 10.1007/3-540-44463-7_15 26, 43

B. Mobasher, H. Dai, T. Luo, and M. Nakagawa. Effective Personalization Based on Association Rule Discovery from Web Usage Data. In *Proc. of the 3rd ACM Workshop on Web Information and Data Management*, pages 9–15, 2001a. DOI: 10.1145/502932.502935 37

B. Mobasher, H. Dai, T. Luo, and M. Nakagawa. Improving the Effectiveness of Collaborative Filtering on Anonymous Web Usage Data. In *Proc. of the Workshop on Intelligent Techniques for Web Personalization*, pages 53–60, 2001b. 25, 31, 32, 44

B. Mobasher, H. Dai, T. Luo, and M. Nakagawa. Effective Personalization Based on Association Rule Discovery from Web Usage Data. In *Proc. of the 3rd ACM Workshop on Web Information and Data Management*, pages 9–15, 2001c. DOI: 10.1145/502932.502935 18, 36, 65

B. Mobasher, H. Dai, T. Luo, and M. Nakagawa. Discovery and evaluation of aggregate usage profiles for web personalization. volume 6, pages 61–82, 2002. DOI: 10.1023/A:1013232803866 18

M. Pazzani and D. Billsus. Learning and Revising User Profiles: The Identification of Interesting Web Sites. *Machine Learning*, 27(3):313–331, 1997. DOI: 10.1023/A:1007369909943 34

M. J. Pazzani. A Framework for Collaborative, Content-Based and Demographic Filtering. *Artif. Intell. Rev.*, 13(5-6):393–408, 1999. DOI: 10.1023/A:1006544522159 56

M. J. Pazzani and D. Billsus. Content-Based Recommendation Systems. In Peter Brusilovsky, Alfred Kobsa, and Wolfgang Nejdl, editors, *The Adaptive Web: Methods and Strategies of Web Personalization*, pages 325–341. Springer, 2007. 33

J. R. Quinlan. Induction of Decision Trees. *Machine Learning*, 1(1):81–106, 1986. DOI: 10.1007/BF00116251 34

D. Raggett, I. Jacobs, and A. Le Hors. HTML 4.01 Specification, 1999. URL http://www.w3.org/TR/REC-html40/. 6

P. Resnick and H. R. Varian. Recommender Systems. *Commun. ACM*, 40(3):56–58, 1997. DOI: 10.1145/245108.245121 1

B. Sarwar, G. Karypis, J. Konstan, and J. Reidl. Item-Based Collaborative Filtering Recommendation Algorithms. In *Proc. 10th Int. World Wide Web Conf.*, pages 285–295, 2001. DOI: 10.1145/371920.372071 32, 33

J. Ben Schafer, Dan Frankowski, Jon Herlocker, and Shilad Sen. Collaborative Filtering Recommender Systems. In P. Brusilovsky, A. Kobsa, and W. Nejdl, editors, *The Adaptive Web: Methods and Strategies of Web Personalization*, pages 291–324. Springer Verlag, 2007. 30, 31

F. Sebastiani. Machine Learning in Automated Text Categorization. *ACM Comput. Surv.*, 34(1): 1–47, 2002. DOI: 10.1145/505282.505283 5

N. Shivakumar and H. Garcia-Molina. Finding Near-Replicas of Documents and Servers on the Web. In *Proc. Int. Workshop on the World Wide Web and Databases*, pages 204–212, 1998. 21

M. Spiliopoulou, B. Mobasher, B. Berendt, and M. Nakagawa. A Framework for the Evaluation of Session Reconstruction Heuristics in Web-Usage Analysis. *INFORMS J. on Comput.*, 15(2): 171–190, 2003. DOI: 10.1287/ijoc.15.2.171.14445 17

J. Srivastava, R. Cooley, M. Deshpande, and P. N. Tan. Web Usage Mining: Discovery and Application of Usage Patterns from Web Data. *ACM SIGKDD Explor. Newsl.*, 1(2):12–23, 2000. DOI: 10.1145/846183.846188 5, 13

F. Tao, F. Murtagh, and M. Farid. Weighted Association Rule Mining Using Weighted Support and Significance Framework. In *Proc. 9th ACM SIGKDD Int. Conf. on Knowledge Discovery and Data Mining*, pages 661–666, 2003. DOI: 10.1145/956750.956836 36

A. Thor and E. Rahm. AWESOME: A Data Warehouse-Based System for Adaptive Website Recommendations. In *Proc. 30th Int. Conf. on Very Large Data Bases*, pages 384–395, 2004. 59

L. Ungar and D. Foster. Clustering Methods for Collaborative Filtering. In *Proc. of the Workshop on Recommendation Systems*, pages 60–64, 1998. 32

C. Wang, J. Lu, and G. Zhang. Mining Key Information of Web pages: A Method and Its Application. *Expert Syst. Appl.*, 33(2):425–433, 2007. DOI: 10.1016/j.eswa.2006.05.017 21

W. Wang and O. R. Zaïane. Clustering Web Sessions by Sequence Alignment. In *Proc. 13th Int. Workshop on Database and Expert Systems Appl.*, pages 394–398, 2002. 49, 51, 52

L. Xiaoli and S. Zhongzhi. Innovating Web Page Classification Through Reducing Noise. *J. Comput. Sci. Technol.*, 17(1):9–17, 2002. DOI: 10.1007/BF02949820 21

L. Yan and C. Li. Incorporating Pageview Weight into an Association-Rule-Based Web Recommendation. In A. Sattar and Ho B. Kang, editors, *Australian Conf. on Artif. Intell.*, pages 577–586. Springer, 2006. 36

O. R. Zaïane. Web Usage Mining for a Better Web-Based Learning Environment. In *Proc. Advanced Technology for Education*, pages 60–64, 2001. 13

O. R. Zaïane, J. Li, and R. Hayward. Mission-Based Navigational Behaviour Modeling for Web Recommender Systems. In *WebKDD*, pages 37–55, 2004. DOI: 10.1007/11899402_3 43

T. Zhang and V. S. Iyengar. Recommender Systems using Linear Classifiers. *J. Mach. Learn. Res.*, 2: 313–334, 2002. DOI: 10.1162/153244302760200641 67

Z. Zhang, J. Chen, and X. Li. A Preprocessing Framework and Approach for Web Applications. *J. Web Eng.*, 2(3):176–192, 2004. 21

B. Zhou, S.C. Hui, and A.C.M. Fong. Web Usage Mining for Semantic Web Personalization. In *Proc. of Workshop on Personalization on the Semantic Web*, pages 66–72, 2005. 61

T. Zhou, Z. Kuscsik, J. G. Liu, M. Medo, J. R. R. Wakeling, and Y. C. Zhang. Solving the Apparent Diversity-Accuracy Dilemma of Recommender Systems. *Proc. of the National Academy of Sciences of the United States of America*, 107(10):4511–4515, 2010. DOI: 10.1073/pnas.1000488107 66

J. Zhu, J. Hong, and J. G. Hughes. PageCluster: Mining Conceptual Link Hierarchies from Web Log Files for Adaptive Web Site Navigation. *ACM Trans. Internet Tech.*, 4(2):185–208, 2004. DOI: 10.1145/990301.990305 39, 40

I. Zukerman, D. W. Albrecht, and A. E. Nicholson. Predicting Users' Requests on the WWW. In *Proc. 7th Int. Conf. on User Modeling*, pages 275–284, 1999. 46

Author's Biography

ŞULE GÜNDÜZ-ÖGÜDÜCÜ

Şule Gündüz-Ögüdücü is an assistant professor at the Department of Computer Engineering, Istanbul Technical University, Turkey. She received her PhD from the same university in 2003. During her doctoral study, she was a visiting research scholar at the University of Waterloo, Waterloo, Canada, in the Database Research Group. In 2003, she won Siemens Excellence award for her PhD thesis. Her research interests are data mining, Web mining, recommender models and folksonomy mining. In these fields, she is a reviewer and co-author of various publications in prestigious journals and international conferences. She is member of IEEE; in 2010, she founded the IEEE Turkey WIE Affinity Group and currently serves as its Chair.

Printed in the United States
by Baker & Taylor Publisher Services